P9-CFV-614

OSCAR ROBERTSON
THE GOLDEN YEAR 1964

ROYALS

MURRAY
OLDERMAN

OSCAR ROBERTSON

THE GOLDEN YEAR 1964

by
Ira Berkow

Murray Olderman
General Editor

PRENTICE-HALL, INC., Englewood Cliffs, N.J.

TO NANCY

Oscar Robertson: The Golden Year 1964
by Ira Berkow

Copyright © 1971 by Ira Berkow

Copyright under International and Pan American
Copyright Conventions

All rights reserved. No part of this book may be
reproduced in any form or by any means, except
for the inclusion of brief quotations in a review,
without permission in writing from the publisher.

ISBN-0-13-642967-X
Library of Congress Catalog Card Number: 76-135400

Printed in the United States of America *T*

Prentice-Hall International, Inc., London
Prentice-Hall of Australia, Pty. Ltd., Sydney
Prentice-Hall of Canada, Ltd., Toronto
Prentice-Hall of India Private Ltd., New Delhi
Prentice-Hall of Japan, Inc., Tokyo

FOREWORD

In the pursuit of writing a book, does an author have to go one-on-one with his subject? If the subject is Oscar Robertson, it doesn't hurt. If the author is Ira Berkow, the physical thesis is feasible. Ira gave away five inches to the Big O, who is 6-5. But Oscar yielded a couple of years, at thirty-two. At any rate, it was a worthwhile exercise of research.

Robertson, of course, is the superfluid star of the Sixties in pro basketball, firmly established as the epitome of excellence. For analogy, what they used to say about Sugar Ray Robinson fits Oscar perfectly: Pound for pound, he is the greatest basketball player in history.

He was the transitional figure in the emergence of the big backcourt playmaker who reduced mere 6-footers to oblivion. For Oscar, not yielding anything in size to the others on the court, surpassed them in grace and movement. And all this came to fruition in the winter of 1963–64, when Oscar broke the grip of the pivot men and won the Podoloff Cup, the National Basketball Association's official symbol for the most valuable player (a center has won it every other year since 1959). That was the Golden Year for the leader of the Cincinnati Royals and forms the backdrop for Berkow's lucid description of the Robertson style.

When he isn't challenging Oscar one-on-one, Ira is the sports editor and columnist for Newspaper Enterprise Association (NEA), a feature service distributed to 700 daily newspapers and the originator of the Podoloff Cup voting for the NBA. Playing basketball at Sullivan High School in his native Chicago gave Berkow the expertise to dissect Oscar as a basketball player (and the guts to face him on the court). But Ira also was interested in Oscar as a complex personality, and this shows through in his book.

As he takes you through Oscar's greatest season, you'll get the feel of what makes this man a champion, the motivational force that produced the No. 1 playmaker in modern basketball.

Murray Olderman
General Editor, Golden Years

PREFACE

On the last night of his first decade in professional basketball, Oscar Robertson stood under the basket in Madison Square Garden and, curiously, clowned a bit. A loose ball rolled his way and Robertson performed the trick of having the ball hop onto his foot, crawl up his leg and nestle into his large hands. Shortly after, teammate Johnny Green prepared to take a nearby jump shot and Robertson hooked arms with the surprised Green and they did a Virginia Reel twirl. Robertson appeared oblivious to the bedsheet banner hanging from the second balcony (or "heaven," as its inhabitants fondly call it) that read: "Hit 'em with your purse, Oscar." Inside the letter *O* a frown was drawn. The most unlikely place for Robertson to demonstrate his sense of humor is on the basketball court, which, for him—like a cathedral to a monk—has been a center of work and worship.

The night was March 21, 1970. After the game Robertson would admit, "Yes, it's a relief that it's over."

Over, it seemed, was Robertson's career with the Cincinnati Royals and perhaps in the National Basketball Association. The bedsheet made reference to it: Two months before this game, Robertson had been informed by the Royals that he would not receive a more attractive contract next season (his yearly salary called for $125,000). In fact, he was told, he had been traded to Baltimore. But a clause in Oscar's contract had given him the right to decide 1) whether he could be traded and 2) if he okayed a trade, the determination of the team.

Robertson chose to stay the season in Cincinnati and much town criticism was brought down on the head of rookie pro coach Bob Cousy, the former Boston Celtic standout playmaker, who said that the Royals simply could not economically afford to keep Robertson. Cousy, however, reiterated his public position that Robertson was one of the best allaround basketball players ever. Despite this kind afterthought, the relationship between Cousy and Robertson became, at its most cordial, polemically distant.

Now, at the end of a decade, Robertson could look back on a career marked by great success, wealth and fame, but also much frustration. Not only had he never played with a championship team, but now he felt unwanted by the Royals.

Cousy's pattern of offense meant that Robertson no longer controlled the ball 90 percent of the time. And too often rookies like Norm Van Lier and Herm Gilliam brought the ball down and seemed to give it up only under duress. There was a sense of youthful indifference, however unintentional, for the star veteran who stood and watched as his heirs dribbled, dribbled, dribbled. Then one day Robertson came to practice at Cincinnati Gardens and the parking-lot attendant asked him why the ad in the morning paper did not have his picture with the rest of the team? That was the first Robertson had heard about it. The Royal front office said it was a mere oversight. A few days later they told him he had been traded.

So this was Robertson's last game for the Royals (he said he would definitely not return to them and also opened possibilities for his entering the rival American Basketball Association—"wherever the money's the best"). Although the game meant nothing in the standings, since Cincinnati had been eliminated from playoff contention and the New York Knicks had clinched first place in the Eastern Division, the game was still important to Robertson.

The game was important because it was a game and because Robertson must continue to prove that he is still Oscar Robertson, the best. It was a "typical Oscar game," as that kind of performance has come to be known: 29 points, 11 rebounds, 7 assists. He took 14 shots from the field and hit on 9—on jump shots in which he somehow hangs in the air until his leaping defender drops from exhaustion and gravity, on shots in which he drives up the middle and leaves his feet only at the last instant when he knows he has no one to pass to and puts it up himself over a Willis Reed and on shots in which he darts a sharp head fake and then skirts a Walt Frazier.

Watching him do that, the Maurice Stokes Benefit basketball game the previous August in the Catskills was recalled. During half time, Robertson had made only two baskets against Frazier.

"I haven't done a thing against Frazier," Robertson told Bud Olsen, a former Royal teammate.

"No disgrace," said Olsen, "Frazier's a helluva defensive player."

"We'll see," said Robertson.

At the start of the second half, Robertson scored three straight baskets on Frazier.

The last game of the decade was "typical' also in that Robertson hollered at a teammate to cut, shouted at the Knicks' Dick Barnett to "Get your hands off me" while being guarded, and threw up his palms and shook his head around at a referee's call. Robertson still wanted to win, fiercely.

This book concerns that drive to play to a peak. It concerns Robertson's ten-year career but is narrowed down to one season, 1963–64, which was his finest for many reasons, and his team's finest. And it concerns universal dilemmas: to try to do more than one can, to seek more than there is and to try to fit one's dream into one's reality.

Ira Berkow
New York City

Shortly after the conclusion of the 1969–70 season, Robertson was traded from the Royals to the Milwaukee Bucks. The Bucks already had Lew Alcindor, the celebrated 7-foot center. The combination of two such eminent players, Alcindor and Robertson, is all that is needed to make a championship team, according to some. Others wondered if a town could be big enough for the two stars, before they went their individual ways. But Alcindor was the good big man that Robertson always said was needed for a championship. Robertson would be going into his 11th NBA season. He knew he had few good seasons left. He knew that if he couldn't win now, with Alcindor, he would never be on a championship team in the NBA.

1

It was the pinnacle of Oscar Robertson's career, it was the abyss. The 1963-64 National Basketball Association season ended with Robertson being voted by rival players the most valuable player in the league. He had been the most valuable player in the midseason All-Star game; he had led the league in assists and in free-throw percentage, and was second to Wilt Chamberlain in scoring. But years later, Robertson would curl a lip and say, "I don't like to talk about that season. It makes me angry just to think about it. We had the best team in the NBA. And we blew the championship." The Royals, at least for the rest of the decade, would never again come as close to a championship.

It was a season of high promises. Favorable winds had begun blowing the season before, 1962-63, when the Royals had caused a flutter in the NBA playoffs. They had finished third in the Eastern Division during the regular season and had upset Syracuse in the first round of the playoffs before going tuck and nip with the Boston Celtics in the division finals.

The Celtics were considered as invincible in their time as the New York Yankees, Notre Dame, Alexander the Great and Perry Mason in theirs. But the Royals, with Robertson the star, battled Boston to the seventh and final game before losing.

This momentum was carried over into the 1963-64 season. And there were reasons for further optimism. The Royals had a new coach, Jack McMahon, fiery and florid-faced. There was still some confusion as to who owned the team, but it seemed that Warren Hensel would soon snip the remaining loose threads and take over the club and provide the decisive administrative leadership it had lacked.

Also, much hullabaloo greeted the coming of a rookie, Jerry Lucas, with knees that were tender, a shooting touch that was delicate and rebounding skills that were ferocious. It was believed that the Royals needed only a good big man to round out a championship team, and Lucas seemed to be that man. Lucas, wrote *Sports Illustrated*, "has aroused more genuine interest among basketball fans than any first-year player in history."

And of course there was Oscar Robertson.

Ask Bill Russell or Bob Pettit or anyone else whose opinion you respected in basketball and the response would be that no one—not now, not ever—could perform on a basketball court with as much overall skill as Oscar Robertson.

"Oscar," said Pettit, "gets my vote for the best all-around player ever."

"He is," said Bob Cousy, "the greatest all-around player to come down the pike in my lifetime."

"He should have been named Dr. Naismith," said Bob Boozer, onetime Royal teammate of Robertson's. (Naismith invented the game.)

After a long holdout one year, Robertson reported thicker than usual around the middle and the rump. The Royals played the Celtics in a preseason game and Robertson scored over 20 points in this his first game back, as opposed to his average of over 30. After the game, Bill Russell said, "A fat Oscar is almost human."

And McMahon, who went on to coach Oscar for several years, delighted in telling the joys of his job. "It's always a pleasure to go to a game or a practice," he said, "because if you love this game as much as I do, it's a thrill to see the best. Oscar is the best."

"I would pay money," said Alex Hannum, then coach of the San Francisco Warriors, "to watch Oscar Robertson play basketball alone."

Not only was Robertson awesome to the opposition and a boon to his teammates and to the boxoffice, but he also had a therapeutic effect on at least one fan: A doctor in Cincinnati, who had a crippling arthritis, said that the only time he did not experience pain was when he sat in Cincinnati Gardens and watched Robertson play basketball.

The grace, the elegance, the precision, the control, the effectiveness with which Robertson performed were appreciated by a gal who knew little about basketball but precious much about beauty of movement. Suzanne Farrell, Cincinnati-born, became one of the world's great ballerinas and the star of the New York State Theatre Company of Lincoln Center. There is an entry in her diary that reads: "We went to see the Royals vs. the Knicks. The 'Big O' was his usual magnificent self. The Royals won 124-118."

Robertson was now twenty-four years old. He was entering his fourth season in professional basketball and, as an

3

individual performer, was about to reach his peak in a career that was remarkable for, among other things, a staccato consistency of excellence.

At 6-5, 200 pounds, he would come slowly onto the court for pregame warmup drills, and he and his reflection in the immaculate blond-wood court would move without a trace of extra motion but with an aura of purpose. One could anticipate another sweet night.

His scooped nose, almost clownish, and his round cheeks, quite boyish, gave a misleading impression of his sense of dedication. The eyes in his milk-chocolate face were alert. Yet he would take lazy dribbles in the layup drill and casually bounce the ball off the backboard and through the corded basket. The juggernaut drive was bottled now, soon to be uncorked. He would walk easily, confidently back to the rebound line with a stride that is not dissimilar to the stroll of a child with an overload of diaper.

Robertson was already the league's top playmaker, even before Cousy retired. He was one of the few guards with the temerity to drive against a Russell or a Chamberlain, and the skill to score. He could shoot over smaller guards, dribble around larger ones, swing a meaningful hip and rebound against almost anyone (he was the club's leading rebounder in 1961-62); he could hit a teammate with a pass when there was only a crack of breath between receiver and defender, was cagey and light-fingered on defense.

In Cincinnati there was buoyant anticipation for the 1963-64 Royals. More people there were paying more money for professional basketball seats than ever before. Advance season-ticket sales were $110,000, some $20,000 more than the Royals' record set in 1960, Robertson's rookie year. This ticket sale was unusual on two counts. First, much of the discussion about basketball was taking place while the time-honored Reds were still ripe in season (and basketball,

4

until Robertson entered the University of Cincinnati in 1956, was not in the vocabulary of many townsfolk; others, who still live in Red Stockings legend, consider basketball only a necessary evil for wintertime exercise). Second, Cincinnatians are not famous for parting with a sports dollar. It was said that ticket-sellers at the Crosley Field bleacher wickets would pry dollar bills loose from a fan only by unbinding one finger at a time.

Tom Grace, who was then executive vice-president of the Royals, said, "When people here go to a racetrack, they head straight for the $2 window."

The players, too, were imbibing this enthusiasm. "We are," said center Wayne Embry, "the best team in professional basketball." (The Royals were not the only ones to be thinking such thoughts. John Havlicek of the Celtics had told Lucas, his former Ohio State teammate, that "the Royals were the best team in the NBA at the end of last season.")

No one wanted a championship more than Oscar Robertson. Ever since his college days at Cincinnati, he had carried a burden. His physical talents as a basketball player were uncontested. His team leadership and influence have been attacked, however. During three years of varsity play, Robertson was named the nation's outstanding college player, and during each season he was the nation's leading scorer. Both accomplishments were unprecedented. But his team never won the NCAA championship. The Bearcats lost in the second round in Robertson's sophomore year, and were defeated in the semifinals the next two seasons. After Robertson had graduated in 1960, Cincinnati won two straight NCAA titles and missed a third in an overtime loss in the 1963 finals.

Robertson learned what it was like to be a winner in high school, at Crispus Attucks in Indianapolis. In his junior and senior years he was the star of a team that won 45 straight games and two state championships, the first school in basketball-mad Indiana to go through a season undefeated and the first school in America with an all-black enrollment to win an open state basketball championship.

After the 1955 championship, Oscar recalls, "It was a great thrill. When the game ended, the local fire department was there with the fire truck, and we all got aboard and rode through town with the siren going, and then we had a bonfire and everything. It was sort of inspiring. It really was."

The next season, in the championship game, Oscar made eighteen baskets (including one from half-court as the game ended) for 39 points. Not long afterward, much of the pure fun of basketball diminished for Robertson, as it does for so many other star high school athletes, badgered and cajoled and enticed by college recruiters competing against each other like a flock of traveling Bible salesmen in a town with only one Christian.

And if the athlete is black like Oscar, sensitive and proud like Oscar, temperamental and talented like Oscar, then when he is treated as an object—as a performer (by the students), as a ruby in a bellybutton (by boastful alumni), as a source of financial gain (for school administrators) and, surely, in a town that is geographically Northern but often characteristically Southern, he was, to some, simply that "moody nigger who can jump like a monkey."

"On the campus," he once said as a college senior, "people would come up to me. They say they want to say hello. They say they just want my autograph, to just talk to me. They want to talk to me because I'm a basketball player. Suppose I was a ditchdigger. Why don't they like me just because I'm Oscar Robertson? But people don't act that way. They wouldn't talk to Oscar Robertson the ditchdigger.

"People are phony. This town is phony. This campus is

6

phony. Don't get me wrong. I've got nothing against Cincinnati, the town or the college. It's no different here than anywhere else—New York, Boston. It's all the same. People are the same everywhere. Phony.

"I've got this far and now all I want to do is get it over with. In June it'll be finished. I can hardly wait."

There was at once an insight and a naïveté in that utterance. He was learning that some people were showering him with adulation not to exalt him but to lift themselves vicariously through him. It was a bitter lesson for the young man from the ghetto.

He was naïve, though, in his one-lump generalization. If he meant "all people are phony," then he would be including himself. And Oscar, as virtually everyone who has met him agrees, is sincere, unaffected, upright, forthright and driven. These are the qualities that set him apart, and these are the qualities that get him in trouble.

Oscar gripes. Often. On the court, the skirl of a referee's whistle will lift his eyebrows, flap his wrists and waggle his tongue. ("Dammit, what's going on around here?" he'll ask.) A teammate who forgets to hustle will get his hide scorched by Oscar's invective. "He's the greatest player there is," said one teammate on the 1963-64 team, "but he is also brash, intolerant and a dictator on the court."

Oscar, though, gets angriest at himself. Andy Cox, the Royals' publicity director in the late Sixties, recalled his first exposure to this facet of Robertson. Cox was seated near the Royals' bench. There was a time-out. Robertson came back steaming to the huddle, pounding a fist in a palm.

"Gee," said Cox, "who's Oscar giving hell to?"

"To himself," Cox was told. "He's just missed two straight shots."

Off the court, he is a respected NBA player representative.

He is quick to complain about pension plans, television rights and travel accommodations, and he has forced results. He is also an aware and outspoken civil rights advocate. Though he says he is no crusader, he has a profound interest in standing up for that cause. "I know a lot of things are wrong, but I can't change the world," he has said. His personal hero is former baseball player Jackie Robinson. "He did something few of us could have done. He took a horrible beating for the sake of a principle and all of us gained by it. Every Negro in America owes him a debt of gratitude."

Robertson is a perfectionist, as involved in practice as in a game. He is equally relentless off the court. Like all perfectionists, he is often gloomy, for unfortunately one cannot paint a masterpiece every evening, nor win a championship each spring. "In life," Robertson once said, "there is not very much to be happy about."

Yet Robertson can often see humor in the most unexpected situations. One night, for example, the team was in a bus returning from a preseason game in Kentucky. Robertson looked out the window and saw a sign with the name of the town they were passing through: WHITESVILLE. "Hey," said Robertson, "what am I doing in a place like *this*."

In the two years preceding Robertson's appearance on the Royals, the team was last in its division, with a record of 19 wins and 53 losses in 1959 and 19 wins, 56 losses the following season. When Robertson joined the club, they won almost as many games (33) in one season as they had in the previous two. The Royals improved to 43-37 in 1961 and then were 42-38 in 1962.

It seemed that the Royals might now be the team to prevent the Celtics from winning their seventh world championship in eight seasons. It seemed the Royals might just win their first. The Royals were gaining in confidence, experience and talent. And the 1963 playoff against the Celtics, the playoff they came so close to winning, now stood Russell-tall in their memories.

2

There was the eerie, lonely, hollow bouncing of the ball on the Boston Gardens floor. In a sweatsuit in the dusky semi-darkness, Sam Jones, alone all afternoon, dribbled, stopped, shot again and again and again.

It was April 10, 1963, and Jones had an important game that night. Before big games, Jones would often come to the arena early to work up a sweat, work out the kinks and work off the pressure.

And he knew he was in for another pressure night very much like the six previous ones in this Eastern Division championship playoff series against Cincinnati. This was the seventh and last game, the one that would break the

3-3 tie. Jones would have to again guard Oscar Robertson.

The Celtics, at the start, had not been mentally prepared for the Royals. First off, they were sure they would meet Syracuse in the division-championship playoff. (Jones, especially, was rooting for Syracuse to beat Cincinnati for the right to meet the first-place Celtics. "All poor Sam had to do," Bob Cousy has written, "is cover Oscar Robertson, who is their playmaker and their scorer and their rebound man and their general all-around wizard and whirling dervish. Oscar is also an inch taller than Sam and he has the ball probably 80 percent of the time. Guarding him is no worse than taking on a windmill with your bare hands.")

Then, when the Royals beat Syracuse in the division semifinals, the Celtics verged on overconfidence (all, that is, except Sam Jones). The Celtics had beaten the Royals easily over the last few years and it was difficult to jog themselves into acknowledging that now the Royals had, as they say, jelled.

In the first game of the series, Boston blew a 22-point lead at home and lost 135-132. The second game was played in Cincinnati and the Celtics, ahead by 9 points in the first half, nearly lost that one, too. But they came back for a 125-102 victory. Confidence restored, the Celts returned to comfortable Boston Garden with the warm home crowds, the familiar parquetlike court and the triumphant championship flags from previous seasons hanging from the rafters. Of all indignities, the Royals beat them again! And Boston, of all things, was behind in the series to the *Royals*. But Boston won the next two games and needed one more to clinch the division title and get on to more important things, the Western Division champions, either Los Angeles or St. Louis.

The upstart Royals were obstinate. And with Robertson

scoring 36 points, beat the Celtics 109-99 in Cincinnati to force the decisive seventh game. So Sam Jones, that April afternoon, perspired and practiced in the dark, hot arena, alone except for the thump of the ball and the remindful silence of the championship flags overhead.

That night, in a spirited game before a capacity crowd of 13,909, Sam Jones had one of the greatest nights of his career. He scored a career high of 47 points. But if Jones was in full steam at one end of the court, he was getting an equally exhaustive workout at the other end. Robertson was having one of his greatest nights, also. He scored 43 points. It is revealing that Robertson had 22 free-throw attempts (he made 21 of them); it proved that Sam and his teammates were giving chase all night to Oscar darting, dashing, penetrating; when Robertson wasn't scoring or passing off for a score, he was being run over by the Celtics—thus all the time spent on the free-throw line. However, the Celtics, with Bill Russell and Tommy Heinsohn and Bob Cousy and K. C. Jones and Frank Ramsey and Satch Sanders and, of course, Sam Jones, were in the end too much for the still-maturing Royals. Boston won 142-131.

("When we finally got out of the Cincinnati series," Cousy said, "poor Sam was so happy at getting rid of Oscar that he almost cried.")

Though they lost to Boston, it was a hellish good way for the Royals to end the season. And for Oscar. It was a year unlike most others for him. In college, and with the Royals in the late Sixties, the irritable question would often arise: Why Can't Oscar Win? Well, in 1962-63, the question was one of amazement: How Did Oscar Almost Win?

Looking back on it years later, Robertson would say, "That season gave me more inner satisfaction than any other. You have to evaluate the team situation and analyze the player personnel. And then consider what we accomplished."

It was a year in which there was a minimum of murmured discussion that Robertson had the ball too much. Each Royal seemed to be giving everything he could. Important, too, was that the team had been fairly stable for the last few years and thus were getting to know each other's moves, speed, abilities. "It takes years of playing together," said Robertson, "for a team to be of championship caliber."

And now Arlen (Bucky) Bockhorn and Oscar at the guards, Wayne Embry at center and Jack Twyman and Bob Boozer at the forwards, were developing into a smooth unit, with Adrian (Odie) Smith and Tom Hawkins coming off the bench as top substitutes. Several other teams had better man-for-man personnel. The Royals, for example, had no center the size or likes of Russell or Chamberlain, though Embry, at 6-8, 250, could walk into the wall and the wall would be the worse for it. And they did not have the balance of the Celtics or the Lakers—with Elgin Baylor, Jerry West, Dick Barnett, Rudy LaRusso—or the St. Louis Hawks—with Bob Pettit, Cliff Hagan, Richie Guerin, Lennie Wilkens, Zelmo Beaty.

But they were solid and getting better. And they were happy together. There was an understandable lightness the night after the sixth game of the Celtic series, which they won at Cincinnati to force the deciding seventh game.

They were convinced now that they were "heir apparent," as some sportswriters termed it, to the Boston dynasty. And maybe now they were creating one of their own. That day, Warren Hensel, bespectacled and bold, who owned only a small part of the team, announced that all arrangements and negotiations had been completed for his taking over club ownership. (He had made himself known to several of the players and coach Charlie Wolf when he offered advice in rather stentorian tones from his courtside seat as a game progressed. And for some reason he seemed to fancy himself Odie Smith's on-court mentor.)

Well, the night after that joyous sixth game, Hensel threw a team party in his home in suburban Cincinnati to celebrate the victory and his new station. The Royals were relaxed as they drove out in several cars. They had nothing to do but enjoy themselves now, since the final Celtic game was three days away. Everyone was relaxed, except Robertson. Yvonne, his wife, noticed that all the other players were wearing neckties. So, while driving out to the Hensel home, Yvonne recommended that Oscar get a tie from Warren. Oscar did a certain amount of harumphing.

Yvonne has the respect of everyone who knows them. She is a former first-grade public school teacher and has a master's degree from Columbia University. She is a vivacious and lovely lady and, as Oscar knows, a woman of taste. ("It says something about the man," said Embry of Robertson, "when you know the kind of woman he married.") Robertson is meticulous about his appearance, as he is about all other personal matters, on and off the basketball court. Embry calls him "style-conscious." And now Yvonne had planted a gnawing thought.

"Oscar," recalls Embry, "was wearing avocado-gold pants, avocado-olive sport jacket, yellow shirt open at the collar. He and Warren went upstairs to the bedroom to select a tie. Well, I mean, Warren's taste in clothes runs, you might say, more conservatively.

"The closest match Oscar could get was a black-and-gray tie. Let's just say it wasn't the perfect match. We were all in the living room, the whole team and our wives, when Oscar came downstairs. I looked up and nearly fell off my chair. I said, 'And now, ladies and gentlemen, we'll have a fashion show. And here, gliding into the room, is our top model—Mister Oscar Robertson. He is wearing the latest avocado-olive sport jacket, avocado-gold pants, yellow shirt, black alligator shoes and'—and then I cleared my throat—'and that *black* tie.' I'm telling you, the place broke up."

Robertson and Embry were roommates for six years, from the time Robertson joined the Royals until Embry left the club in 1966. "Whenever you would see O," said teammate Tom Hawkins, "you would see Embry, and whenever you'd see Embry you would see O."

The two were different in many ways, though it seemed to cement their friendship rather than split it. Embry, for example, was more extravertial and was winsome about personal belongings. This led to much ribbing.

"I remember," said Odie Smith, "that Oscar always needled Embry about his car. Wayne would have all kinds of junk on the seats. Oscar's car was always clean as a whistle."

That night at Hensel's home, Robertson was warmly embarrassed by Embry's formal presentation as he entered the living room, so he sought revenge the rest of the evening.

Hensel's dog took a liking to Embry and sat at his feet. When Embry rose, the dog trotted after him with chummy yips. Embry could not shake the animal.

"Well," Oscar announced, "it looks like Wayne found a long-lost relative."

There were some chuckles, though nothing to match the belly laugh on Oscar the sartorial model. Robertson, with customary tenacity, continued to wreak vengeance. When Embry sat in a large chair, which barely accommodated him, the chair squeaked when he shifted.

"Embry broke the chair," said Robertson to everyone, ratting on his pal with glee. "He broke it."

15

3
❧

Robertson was the last Royal to sign his contract for the 1963-64 season. He is usually the last to sign. He has often missed several weeks of training camp, and once waited until two days before the regular season began to agree to salary terms. This time Robertson and his lawyer J. W. (Jake) Brown—a pleasant fellow and rugged bargainer, a man who has Robertson's confidence, respect and friendship (and the feelings are mutual in all respects)—this time they deliberated until the opening day of training camp for veteran players, September 15th.

When Robertson joined the Royals as a rookie, three years before, he had accepted a three-year $100,000 contract that included bonus clauses based on attendance. With that contract having run its course, Robertson now received an estimated $50,000-a-year contract and became, next to Frank Robinson—who was earning nearly $100,000 a year with the Reds, Cincinnati's second-highest-paid athlete.

Robertson knows his value to the team and has always demanded what he considered payment in kind. Surprisingly, one point that seemed to be against him was his almost mechanical, consistent brilliance on the court.

"They expect a lot from me," said Robertson. "When I get 30 points, 10 assists and 10 rebounds, they talk about somebody who got 17 points when no one expected it from him. They say, 'Oh, Robertson. Yeah. He played his usual game.' But if that's my usual game, then let them pay me for it. What else could I do for them? Sell popcorn? Sweep the floor? Do handstands?"

Bill Mokray, former Celtic promotional director and one-time compiler of the annual NBA record book, put Oscar and his salary discussions in perspective when he said: "There is an axiom in professional sports that the least expensive player on a team is usually the highest salaried." He went on to use Robertson as an illustration to prove his point: The Royals lost $108,997 during the 1958-59 season and $40,654 the next. Then Robertson joined the team. Attendance rose to 207,020 and the Cincinnati Royals showed a profit for the first time since the invention of the wheel.

Pepper Wilson, affable, bald and pipe-smoking, was then the Royals' general manager and the person who worked out salary terms with Robertson and Brown. At the mention of Brown, a grimace courses the length of Wilson's lips. Wilson is the first to give credit, however grudgingly, for negotiating skill.

As for Oscar, Wilson says simply, "He is a thoroughbred. Like all thoroughbreds, he's a bit highstrung. But he is no prima donna. When you come down to it, he really hasn't been that difficult to negotiate with."

In years to come, Oscar would be one of the few professional athletes to earn $100,000 a year. He was once asked if this kind of salary was not disproportionate to what an athlete contributes to society. A schoolteacher, for example, who is supposed to be shaping the minds of the future will make 90 percent less than someone who runs around half-naked chasing a round ball before 10,000 or so spectators.

"You should be paid what you deserve," said Robertson. "It is a matter of supply meeting demand. If there is a demand for basketball talent, and if you are talented, then you should be paid accordingly.

"The important point is talent. Not all basketball players should be paid the same. Just as all schoolteachers should not be paid the same. The good ones should get more than the mediocre. Tell me how some schoolmarm who has been doing the same thing for forty years is as valuable as a teacher who is with the times? People tend to group teachers and truckdrivers and scientists and athletes and others so they all come out alike. They shouldn't."

Robertson, however, said that he often does think that playing basketball is a waste of time. "I think about it all the time," he said. "I think, 'What will these fifteen years of playing basketball mean when I'm in business in years to come? What was my schooling for, anyway?' "

The thought of a silly and prodigal manhood haunts athletes. One, Al Kaline, the Detroit Tiger baseball player, said he has often mulled the same problem. "I often think," said Kaline, "that I should have contributed more to society. I don't know, maybe I would like to have been a doctor. But that's all in the past. Now I'll sit in the dugout and look out on the field and think to myself, 'Well, you're a performer and if you can maybe inspire a few kids or give some relief from daily tensions to some of the fans, well, then my life is worthwhile.' "

And, so the story goes, philosopher Herbert Spencer said to a young man who had just beaten him at billiards: "Moderate skill, sir, is the sign of a good eye and a steady hand, but skill such as yours argues a youth misspent."

Essayist I. A. Williams commented on this (without considering that, just possibly, Spencer was a sore loser): "Is any game worth playing supremely well, at the price of constant practice and application? Against the professional player I say nothing; he is a public entertainer, like any other, and by his skill in his particular sport he at least fulfills the first social duty of man—that of supporting himself and his family by his own legitimate exertions."

Even the most fish-eyed skeptic would have to admit that, if Mr. Williams is correct, then Robertson is a bread-winner of the highest order.

For all athletes, the pall of a comparatively brief athletic career hangs over them. They know that they must extract as much out of management as possible. Management, aware that the athlete's threats of holdout usually have as much substance as the wind, handles negotiations with a velvet-covered iron fist. The athlete, in the end, must capitulate, or lose a season, and each of his seasons are precious indeed. For every year the muscles grow older, the reflexes slower.

4

Robertson found training camp different this time. It was held in the same place, Lockbourne Air Base, forty miles north of Columbus. But there was a new coach, Jack Mc-Mahon, and an important new player, Jerry Lucas.

Rookie camp had been held the week before and from the dozen or so trying out, the only players retained were Lucas and Jay Arnette, who had spent three previous years in the Los Angeles Dodgers' baseball farm system; Mack Herndon, a forward from Bradley University; Joe Roberts, who had played one year with Lucas at Ohio State and now was on trial loan from the Philadelphia 76ers; and Bud Olsen, a rookie the year before but had played so little that Mc-Mahon considered him a rookie in experience.

Otherwise, there were the familiar faces: Smith, Bockhorn, Boozer, Embry, Hawkins and Twyman. There was a new atmosphere, however. There was hope and expectation after last season's dashing finish. And there was curious anticipation concerning McMahon and Lucas.

McMahon was an outstanding pro guard with the old Rochester Royals (where, in 1955, his roommate was a rookie named Jack Twyman) and with the St. Louis Hawks. Before that he was an All-American at St. John's. Brooklyn was where McMahon was born and raised. As a professional guard he was considered steady but unspectacular. He was always in the shadow of other guards on the same team. At Rochester he had played behind Bob Davies and Bobby Wanzer, two excellent players. At St. Louis, where he started, he helped the Hawks win the world championship in 1958. But his running mate, Slater Martin, received the bulk of the praise.

Med Park, a former Hawk guard who was second-string in that championship year, has contended that McMahon was an unselfish player who "gave the ball up to Pettit, Hagan and Martin," the three who did the big scoring. "Slater is little and flashy and gets the headlines," said Park, "but McMahon is the one who holds them together."

McMahon's eighth and last season as a player was in 1959-60, where he also served as assistant Hawk coach and player-personnel chief. The following season he coached the Kansas City Steers of the American Basketball League to a 58-28 overall record. The Steers won the first- and second-half championships, but were defeated by the Cleveland Pipers in the final playoffs.

Proving his skill in what was considered an inferior league, McMahon was ready for an NBA coaching job. He got one, however short-lived. Frank Lane, the controversial baseball man, was then general manager of the Chicago

Zephyrs, a second-year expansion team, and he knew and respected McMahon. Lane convinced Chicago owners Mort Lubin and Dave Trager that McMahon should be the replacement for Jim Pollard, whose Chicago Packers had stumbled through their first year winning only 18 games out of 70. Changing the name from the Packers to the Zephyrs did not change the caliber of the team. After the Zephyrs' first 38 games, they had won 12—about a 5-percent improvement over the previous year. But it wasn't good enough for Chicago owners and, despite Lane's protests, McMahon was out looking for a new job.

He got the one he wanted the following June.

Warren Hensel was seeking an opportunity to dump Royal coach Charley Wolf. Wolf had been the Royals' coach for the last three years, or ever since Robertson joined the club. Wolf had helped mold the Royals into a team that commanded respect. And the Royals' work in the playoffs against Syracuse and Boston reflected benignly on Wolf. "Wolf's job," wrote a Cincinnati newspaperman at the time, "was applauded throughout the league."

Hensel, however, was not one of those standing on his chair and cheering. He had often been openly critical of Wolf, particularly when Wolf would bench Jack Twyman, who was second only to Robertson in team scoring. Wolf also felt that Hensel would curtail his authority in the area of player personnel. He was certain of it when Hensel went alone to the 1963 postseason league meetings in New York.

The handwriting on the wall was all too obvious to Wolf. It wasn't long before Fred Zollner, owner of the Detroit Pistons, arranged to hire Wolf to replace Dick McGuire. Upon hearing of Wolf's simultaneous resignation and appointment, Hensel said, "This is absolutely perfect for all concerned." Later he added, "Wolf did a good job here.

It was just a case of personalities clashing." When asked which personalities, Hensel replied, "Me, the players and everybody."

Hensel, still a minor stockholder pending agreement on the rental clause of Cincinnati Gardens, was nonetheless the man in charge now. He went after a new coach. Applications were received from Vince Cazzetta and John Castillani, both former Seattle University coaches. Johnny Dee of Notre Dame applied, as did former Piston coach Red Rocha and former NBA star Arnie Risen. Others mentioned for the job were Frank McGuire and Paul Seymour, both former NBA coaches, and Dudley Moore, former Duquesne and La Salle coach. Hensel also received an application from Jack McMahon.

As with all adventurers, there exists in these men an element of the foolhardy. Why does a man want to be a coach or manager of a professional sport? The saying is that they are hired to be fired. Just as the mercenary must surely know that one of these days he will not return from afar, the professional coach knows the guillotine is always poised.

"Every manager knows he will be fired," said Mayo Smith, after his Detroit Tigers won the 1968 World Series. "There were only two that weren't. Connie Mack and Clark Griffith. And they owned the clubs. Why do I manage? Why does anyone manage? Because it's in your blood, I guess. That's all." Smith was fired after the 1970 season.

One man whose blood did not need the injection of coaching a professional basketball team was Ned Wulk. Former coach at Xavier University in Cincinnati and then coach of the nation's third-ranking college team, Arizona State University. Wulk was Hensel's choice to replace Wolf. Wulk turned it down.

So, on June 19, 1963, Jack McMahon signed a one-year contract to coach the Royals. Why McMahon? "McMahon's views," said Hensel at the time, "are similar to mine. I think we can work together." And how did McMahon view the team? "This is the coming club of the NBA," said McMahon upon signing the contract. "It's a young club and they showed they can win. This club has great potential, especially if we can get Lucas and Tom Thacker to go with what we already have." McMahon also said he would like to rest Robertson more, that going at 48 minutes a game every game would eventually hurt his effectiveness. He also wanted more help under the boards to let Oscar, the leading rebounder among NBA guards, concentrate on scoring and setting up the offense.

The Royals were to find that McMahon and Wolf had dissimilar approaches to preparing a team. Wolf had never been exposed to professional basketball before becoming the Royals' coach. He had been plucked from obscure Villa Madonna College in Covington, Kentucky. He was a Cincinnatian and a personable fellow. He grew in popularity with the fans as the team improved, which is the way it usually is. He was not, however, always a hit with his players. At first they resented his inexperience in professional basketball, and it reached boiling points with veterans who were offended by Wolf's strict order, organization and discipline. For example, he insisted on running basic college patterns. The veterans protested that you don't get layups in the NBA. And what kind of college tripe is this? The training rules were rigid. When traveling, the players were required by Wolf to wear neckties and sport jackets. If they goofed off in practice, they ran laps.

Robertson was not exempt from these rules, of course. And he, too, ran enforced laps after practice on occasion. In December of Robertson's rookie year, Wolf told Robertson and Twyman to run 25 laps around the Cincinnati Gardens court because of dull play in practice. Wolf was so stringent that he even refused to allow the players' wives to wear slacks when meeting the team at the airport.

"He didn't exactly say we couldn't cuss in the locker room," recalled one player, "but you kind of felt like you shouldn't."

Despite the griping and frowning, the Royals did show improvement under Wolf. The Royals were considered the best-conditioned team in the NBA. And Wolf's insistence on working for good shots rather than the individualistic run-and-fire style of many NBA teams, contributed to the Royals breaking the league record for field-goal percentage in each of Wolf's three seasons. Of course, it did not hurt to have marksmen like Twyman and Robertson shooting field goals for you.

"Jack," said Jim Schottlekotte, who covered the team for the Cincinnati *Enquirer*, "loosened things up." In fact, McMahon would even go out for a beer with some of the players.

McMahon's first concern was, of course, Lucas. And he was impressed with Lucas right from the start. "Sure, there was still a question as to how Luke would make out as a pro," McMahon would say later, "but he worked so hard in rookie camp that I said to myself, 'He's really going to be something.'"

It had been a long way to Cincinnati for Jerry Lucas. Middletown, Ohio, some forty miles north of Cincinnati, was where Lucas became a household name in Ohio. He was an All-State star on two state class-AA high school championship teams in three years. After scores of college recruiters fell from the sky to try to swoop him off, Lucas decided on Ohio State. Among so many others, U of C fans were disappointed. The Royals, however, felt they would profit anyway. The territorial draft was then in effect. It meant that they had first crack at college players from their vicinity.

Robertson had been a territorial draft choice—and Lucas would be. But after teaming with Havlicek and Larry Siegfried and Mel Nowell, among others, for three Big Ten titles, one NCAA championship and two NCAA second-place finishes (University of Cincinnati had beaten them twice), Lucas had second thoughts about turning pro.

In April 1961, in his junior year, Lucas said, "The physical and mental strain of the NBA game just doesn't seem worth it. I have no desire to join their rat race, playing 80 to 100 games a year and living out of a suitcase. Physically, too, it's a rough game and my knees aren't the best anymore."

Tom Grace said that the Royals, in the summer of 1962, had communicated with Lucas to get him to change his mind, and that an important Royal executive had a golf date with Lucas one day that summer. According to Grace, Lucas had told the executive that he had decided to join the Royals. When the executive arrived home to Cincinnati, a business partner called and said *Sports Illustrated* had just released the story that Lucas had signed a contract with the new Cleveland Pipers of the American Basketball League. It was true.

The Pipers, as it turned out, never played a game. All the while the Piper management was negotiating with the NBA for admission. When it looked like the Pipers, with Lucas the ace in the hole, would join the NBA, Lucas said in November 1962, "I admit I am excited about playing in the best league there is." After a year the NBA, for some reason, no longer appeared to him to be a rat race. Lucas added, "The ill feeling that seems to exist between myself and Cincinnati is there but I didn't create it. The sports-writers there just seemed to feel resentment toward me when I chose to attend Ohio State." If Lucas had stopped there he would have been just a man with an opinion. But he went one step further and turned himself into a bad prophet.

"I will never play for Cincinnati anymore," he added, "and I think they [the sportswriters] finally realize it." Later that month the Pipers, unexpectedly, were refused an NBA franchise. In January the league folded. Seven months later, on August 19, Jerry Lucas, with flashbulbs bursting, smilingly, delightedly, enthusiastically signed a contract to play for the Cincinnati Royals.

("He has a space between his teeth and when he smiled that way, lifting his eyebrows, his black, deeply set eyes glittering, he looks like Terry Thomas at his most diabolical," wrote Leonard Shecter in *Sport* magazine.)

"I'm glad to join the Royals," said Lucas. "Basketball is my life and I had a yearning to be back. I will move my family here and make Cincinnati my home. I'm looking forward to playing with Oscar. I only hope that I can help Oscar and the Royals."

Following the press conference, Pat Harmon, sports editor for the Cincinnati *Post*, wrote, "If Lucas is half the player his rookie season that Oscar was in his, the Royals should be satisfied." Harmon added, with solid good sense, "There is an image of animosity between Lucas and the city of Cincinnati, but Lucas will be like any other pro athlete. He can play himself into popularity. If he stars for the Royals, he'll be a favorite here."

"He just could make us a winner," said Hensel.

There was some discussion about Lucas's weak knees, but Jerry said that the year's layoff had helped strengthen them, since he'd exercised with heavy weights and hadn't exposed them to the rigorous pounding of the court. He would have to play forward with Cincinnati, yet all his life he had been a center. Could he adjust? He thought he could.

Robertson and Lucas were familiar with each other. They had been on the 1960 United States Olympic team (coincidentally, so had Royal teammates Boozer, Smith and Arnette). So their style of play would not be totally new to each other. A larger question, perhaps, was how they would respond to each other personally. A friction between them might be as harmful to the team as their physical talents could be beneficial. It seemed that much of the relationship would be up to Robertson, the established veteran, the acknowledged star, who controlled the ball nearly 80 percent of the time for the Royals.

"I don't foresee any problems because Jerry is a very fine team player," said Robertson. "I played with him in the Olympic Trials and in the Olympics. He has a knack of knowing what to do with the ball when he's tied up. This makes a big difference. On any winning team the teamwork is what does it."

Robertson conceded that Lucas's presence might cut into his 28.3 scoring average of the year before but added, "I think my job is to keep the team moving and try to hit the open man." At another time, however, Robertson readily admitted, "Though I wish it were different, we still get paid for putting the ball in the basket. So I like to score as well as the next man."

(Interestingly, McMahon, like Robertson, lamented that the more you score in pro ball the more you'll be paid. "You know," said McMahon, years later. "I think Oscar could even have been a better basketball player. That's almost laughable, to think Oscar could have been better. But it's true. You always knew somehow he'd get his 30 points a game. But if he were just to feed, and if there was no record of who made the points, he would have been a better all-around player. But that's the nature of our game. To know who scores. Like the guy who is ready to go out of a game and a replacement is waiting on one knee at the sideline, and the guy in the game takes one last shot. Never could understand that. 'Is it such a big thing for 2 points?' I'd ask.")

"I think all of us were planning on one player, Lucas, to lead us to victory," said Arlen Bockhorn. "And Oscar was, too. He wanted Jerry to do well because Oscar wanted to win."

"We all looked forward to Jerry coming on the team," said Embry. "We felt we would really be good. We were, too."

"There was no jealousy by Oscar," said Hawkins. "No one has ever really posed the threat to O as the greatest player ever. And only Jerry West and Elgin Baylor can even approach him. Oscar wasn't worried about anyone being a better player than him. He just wanted the team to be better. And if Lucas could help, then he wanted to help Lucas."

There would be, however, one distinct and immediate sour point about all this. Lucas, before ever pulling on a pair of Royal shorts, had a starting spot. Years later he would admit that he had some apprehension. "There have been college All-Americans who never made it in the pros," he said. "I had no thoughts different from any other rookies. I just wanted to make the team."

Bob Boozer, who had been a Royal for three years, had been a starter for the past two. Each year he had improved. In scoring his averages increased from 8.4 to 13.7 to 14.3. He had also been the team's second-best rebounder the previous year. But on the day Lucas signed a contract with the Royals, Boozer became a substitute. This disturbed Boozer greatly, of course. It also disturbed Robertson, and it was not unimportant to him that Bob Boozer was a black man.

5

Six thousand people crowded into the Lockbourne gymnasium on September 19, just a few days after the veterans reported, to watch the Royals scrimmage. Many came to see Lucas, including Fred Taylor, Ohio State basketball coach. And what they saw most surely pleased them. Oscar Robertson's gold-shirted team beat Wayne Embry's green shirts 100-70, and, more to the point, Robertson and Lucas, on the same team, worked together smoothly.

Lucas was played at forward by McMahon. In days to come this would vary. Lucas would be sent into the pivot, not so much in hopes of working him in as a center again but to restore his confidence, which would wane after being roughed up by veterans like Bob Pettit.

In this game, Lucas kept cutting for the basket and

Robertson kept whipping passes to him that resulted in scores. Oscar also made 6 of 7 field-goal attempts, prompting McMahon to say, "He was the usual Oscar—running the whole show. I've never seen him better."

As for Lucas, McMahon said, "I think he's going to be a great pro. Good size, rebounds and surprisingly good speed getting downcourt." (To intimates, McMahon confided, "My biggest job is to get the three guys who work the best with Oscar and Luke. After all, just the two of them nearly could beat some teams.")

After that scrimmage, McMahon also mentioned that Mack Herndon had looked good and, though he was 6-5 and had played only forward and center for Bradley, just might work out at guard.

In a scrimmage the following day, Jay Arnette, lean and speedy, worked impressively at guard with Robertson, "But then again," reported the Cincinnati *Enquirer*, "O has a way of making all his teammates go."

At various other times, other guards caught the eye of the coach; it was one more man in the search for three complements for Robertson and Lucas. One day it was Odie Smith, hitting with his uncanny long, looping shot from 18, 20, 25 feet out. Another day it was Joe Roberts, on trial loan from the 76ers. And steadily, efficiently, there was Arlen Bockhorn. Every year, it seemed, he was always fighting for a job. And every year he got it. He had been a Royal starter ever since he joined the team as a rookie out of Dayton in 1958. But he never seemed to have a secure spot no matter how well he performed. Crew-cut, thick-set at 6-4, 200, he was considered one of the most rugged guards in the NBA. And quite possibly it was his lack of finesse that made him appear, in the minds of rivals, someone who could be beaten out. Yet Bockhorn was a good defensive player—his best night probably was when he held Bob Cousy to 4 baskets in 27 attempts. He was also a fine passer and adequate shot, once making eleven-straight field goals in a half. But Bockhorn was now facing one of his stiffest challenges. He had suffered ankle injuries the season before, and though not severe enough to prevent him from playing, they did impede his effectiveness. He had averaged 11.7 points per game, compared with 15.8 the year before. Also, Bockhorn was thirty years old, the oldest member of the team.

Steve Hoffman, then the Royals' publicity director, said, "He had great fervor and was an aggressive player. And every year he would take a rookie apart in camp as if it were a postseason playoff game. But these rookies were a threat to his job. I remember Mike Mendenhall saying, when he was cut from the Royals after a rookie trial, that Bucky killed him for pro ball in two weeks. Bucky would knock his mother down a flight of stairs to keep his job—and everybody liked him."

Robertson also had great respect for Bockhorn, and may have drawn some inspiration from Bockhorn's tenacity. Bockhorn was not gifted like Robertson but played with such heart that he fulfilled his potential. In classrooms, nowadays, that kind of pupil is known as an "overachiever."

"I think," said Bockhorn, "that O and I complemented each other very well. On defense I would usually take the big or tougher guard, the Richie Guerins and Sam Joneses. Those were the guys who might take him inside and maybe get him in foul trouble. But my primary job on a team with Oscar was defense. On offense there is no one like Oscar. In fact, he's the greatest athlete I've ever been associated with. Want to hear something amazing, I don't think that O ever led me with a poor pass on a fast break. That's incredible. And he also helped me indirectly with scoring. I mean, when

33

he was double- and triple-teamed I would be open. And you know with O that as soon as you're open, he'll hit you with the pass.

"It was funny in camp. Sure, I always played as hard as I could against the other guards. And I'd often wear them down. There was one I didn't, though. Oscar. He's a lot stronger than he might appear. And if you'd get him upset, he'd really put it on you. He'd tear you up. He did it to me, more than once."

(Pete Newell, who coached Robertson in the Olympics, was coach of California when he witnessed Robertson get upset with the following results: "We were playing Cincinnati in the NCAA semifinals one year," said Newell. "We scored with 6 seconds left in the half. Our only mistake was that we scored over Oscar. He got the ball out and went through every guy on our team. They were almost lined up in a row. He scored at the buzzer.")

"O never said much to me," said Bockhorn. "That's the way he was, though. But he knew that I was giving 110 percent, that I was playing to the best of my ability. He realized this helped him, too."

Odie Smith was the other veteran guard. He had not played a great deal in his two previous seasons but, with Bockhorn's position unsure, he had a notion he could crack the starting lineup. There is a warmth in Smith's angular face and blue eyes. He seems a man happy to be Odie Smith, happy to be a basketball player, happy, in fact, just to be. And on the court he, like Bockhorn, plays with a driving intensity. To be in the pros, and to be only 6-1, you'd better have that intensity—along with a helluva good outside shot, which is what Smith has. He also demonstrated what is called "grit" in some places but "guts" in the pros. "You have not seen fearlessness," said McMahon, "until you see Odie standing in front of someone and taking an

offensive foul." And when there is someone 6-6 and weigh-
ing 250 pounds bearing down on you, and you don't move
out of the way, "fearlessness" might be just one of the
qualities ascribed to you.

Smith developed his shooting eye in the makeshift basket
in a clearing across the creek from his home in Golo,
Kentucky, in the western part of the state. And the "town"
of Golo, as Smith described it, "has a country store and a
service station." And a basket across the creek from the
Smith farm. Very little else.

Smith also had the name "Odie" pinned on him during
his high school days. He and his brother Ed were called
Odie and Pappy after Grand Ole Opry radio stars of Nashville, Tennessee. Whenever he was called Odie, Adrian protested. Whenever Ed was called Pappy, Ed shrugged it off.
So, naturally, the name "Odie" stuck and the name "Pappy"
evaporated.

Adrian Smith was honorable mention all-Kentucky while
playing for Farmington High School. He wasn't 6 feet tall
yet, and the major colleges couldn't see that far down. So
Smith wound up at Northeast Mississippi Junior College.
He averaged 24 points a game for two years there, and had a
high-point game of 48 against Scooba, Mississippi, Junior
College.

Well, Scooba may not have been Tennessee or Georgia,
but it was sufficient for coach Adolph Rupp to bring Smith
back home. At Kentucky, Smith played with the "Fiddlin'
Five" and helped the Wildcats win the 1958 NCAA championship.

In 1959 he played with Robertson, Lucas, Arnette and
Boozer on the U.S. team in the Pan-American Games, which
won the championship, and on the 1960 U.S. Olympic team,
which won the gold medal.

When Smith was at Kentucky the Royals put him on their

negotiations list. But they did little negotiating, as it turned out. And three years later, after Smith had spent two years in the army and another year with the Akron Goodyears of the National Industrial Basketball League, he sent the Royals a letter asking if they remembered him and if they did would they please give him a few minutes of their time so he could show them he knew what a jump shot was? They agreed. And this time the player, Odie, stuck.

In his rookie season, Smith averaged 7.2 points per game, and he raised that to almost 9 a game the following season. The highlight of his career came near the end of 1963 when he scored 22 points in the playoffs against Boston.

Surprisingly, after Embry left in 1966, Robertson was to become closer to Smith than to any other Royal. It was surprising on two counts. Firstly, Smith is white and looks and sounds like deep Kentucky, though his admiration and respect for Robertson the man and Robertson the athlete broke down whatever barriers there might have been, if, indeed, there ever were any. Secondly, Smith was the target of much criticism by Robertson on the court. Robertson has always lit the fire under the other players on his team. He has done it by his performance, by his passing, by his sharp tongue when a teammate fails to move a step closer for a shot, is not awake for a pass, falls down on defense. Oscar is the leader, he feels that's his job. He ignites with his criticisms, to be sure, but he has also burned a player now and then. And, at first, he burned Smith. Robertson seemed to be on Smith more than on others. ("It always seemed," said Arnette, "that O expected more out of Odie, for some reason.")

"Now," said Smith, a few years later, "I know it was for my own good. I didn't know what I could expect from him. He's so good, sometimes he throws passes you can't handle, or you're not ready for. Anything he said to me was right.

And he's treated me just great. He tells me, 'Take your shot. You're one of the best shooters on the team. You ought to shoot more.'"

(As years went by, Robertson publicly praised Smith for the way he worked to improve himself. Their friendship grew.

("He's hard to get to know," Smith said. "But now we confide in each other, and we'll seek advice from each other on business deals. I think he's a fine person. Our wives are also friendly. They sit together at games and talk on the phone. And Paula, my wife, made a baby shower for the Robertson's third child. O never said a thing about it to me, but I know he appreciated it.")

In rookie camp, there were six guards, but only Jay Arnette would make the club. Arnette had been in 1960 the Royals' second draft choice, after Robertson. He had been an All-American basketball player at the University of Texas and was on the 1960 Olympic team. But instead of trying to make the Royals upon his return, he accepted a $20,000 bonus contract from the Los Angeles Dodgers. After three years in the minor leagues, Arnette felt he was not progressing as he'd hoped he would. He was a centerfielder and had been dropped from Class-AA Texas League ball at Albuquerque, New Mexico, to the Class-A Pioneer League at Great Falls. At Great Falls he hit .295, his best pro average. Spokane of the Class-AAA Pacific Coast League had offered him a contract for the next season. Arnette, though he now saw daylight in his baseball career, was nonetheless tired of the grind of baseball, particularly those interminable, jostling bus rides in the dead of night. So he decided to give pro basketball a try. Whenever possible, as the baseball season drew to a close, he practiced alone in a Great Falls high school gym.

Arnette, with a kindly yet rough-hewn face of the Southwest, under a tangle of curly hair, was exceptionally fast afoot and an extraordinary jumper—at 6-2 he could dunk. He had been clocked as the fastest man in the Dodgers' farm system, running 60 yards in 6.3. And it was his speed on the basketball court that set him apart in the Royals' training camp; it was often as humorous as it was marvelous.

"You'd think he was falling on his face during a fast break," said Steve Hoffman.

"Arnette," McMahon would later say, "was too fast for himself. No one could dribble the ball as fast as he could run. Whoosh. He'd be running and the ball would be behind him."

McMahon, though, liked Arnette's speed and drive and had hopes for his shot. In training camp, Arnette was learning that defense in the pros was much different from that of the Southwest Conference. He was having problems getting his shot off. At Texas he would take a pass and shoot, or shoot off the dribble. Faking was an unnecessary chore.

Arnette watched Robertson work. Oscar's head or shoulder fake could topple a defender on his heels and enable Robertson to sweep around him easily. Or he would dribble in that hard thump-thump manner, then stop and raise only an eyebrow it seemed, yet the defender would soar. As he came down, Robertson would go up for a clear 15-foot jump shot. And Oscar was quick, too, though not as fast as Arnette. Yet, Arnette observed, Robertson was able to take advantage of what he had to a greater extent.

After practice one day, Arnette approached Robertson and asked for some guidance. Arnette had been somewhat apprehensive about it. He did not know how Robertson would react. Arnette had been his teammate in the Olympics, yet he never got to know the rather aloof Robertson as a whole person. And like so many others he had great admiration for him as a basketball player.

"Oscar always gave everything he had to the game," said Arnette. "In training camp he was like a rookie trying to make the club. Like me. I remember the first time I saw him play. It was in the NCAA tournament in Kansas City. He scored 40 points and he made it look so easy. I said, 'Gosh, he's not that good.' Then I played with him in the Olympics and I was amazed at how well he handled the ball, how great his vision is—I mean, he sees everything happening on the court—and his greatest asset is body control. He is never off balance.

"But even in the Olympics he fooled me. He played forward. He did a lot of driving and shooting from in close. And then he went to the pros to play guard. I didn't think he'd play that well. I didn't think he would be an effective outside shooter. Wrong again."

So Arnette approached Robertson for advice. "Oscar," said Arnette, "You've got this fantastic first step with the ball. And I can't shake my man. How do you do it?"

Oscar was pleased and interested.

They stayed after practice. The two of them—and more than once. With the evening shadows slashing through the windows, two figures were silhouetted at the top of the foul circle at one end of the gym. Oscar demonstrated how he uses the left foot as a pivot, gives a quick head fake to the left, then bursts to the right with a swift short step and dribble.

"I tried and tried," said Arnette. "But I just couldn't do it like him."

It is that first step that often puts the defensive man a half-step behind Oscar and leaves him as unfulfilled as a racing greyhound chasing the mechanical rabbit. Robertson has two reasons for that initial explosion.

"There are quite a few players in the NBA faster than me, but I feel confident I can beat anybody if I execute a good fake and beat them with my first step. The best exercise is wind sprints. Wind sprints also help you in your change of pace. A lot of players never take the time to develop that. They move at the same rate of speed all the time, whether they have the ball or not, whether they're on offense or defense. That's just plain silly, because it makes the defensive man's job just that much easier if he can gauge your speed. The idea on offense is to keep the defensive man back on his heels. Keep him reacting and recovering, rather than up on his toes challenging you. The way to do this is by constantly changing speeds."

Secondly, that fast first step comes from so many years of practice that it becomes as reflexive as knowing how to tie a shoelace. Some observers say that a natural athlete—like Robertson—does not have to perfect his skills, since they were sharpened and honed at birth. Ted Williams, the great baseball hitter, once made an interesting comment about this: "People talk about my great eyesight and reflexes as if those were the reasons for my success," said Williams. "That's bullshit. Do you know how I learned to hit a ball? Practice, dammit. Practice, practice, practice, practice! Trial and error. Trial and error. Trial and error!"

No one, as Arnette noted, works harder in practice than Robertson. He has done it ever since he was a kid on the "Dust Bowl" playground in Indianapolis, ever since his high school coach, Ray Crowe, gave him the keys to the school gym so he could practice alone during the summer.

Olympic coach Pete Newell recalls, "There was never the question 'Where's Oscar?' He was always there. He worked as hard in practice as he did in a game."

"Oscar," said Bockhorn, "would get angry if you didn't put out in practice like it was a game. And justifiably so."

"Sure," said Oscar, "I play hard in practice. I feel you'll

do the same in a game. You learn habits. Good ones or bad ones. Look, take a boy who steals. He lives in the streets. Take him off the streets and into a nice environment. After a while he'll be stealing again. It's what you get in the habit of doing. And for me, now, basketball is no longer a fun thing—it's a business. I am very serious about it."

Other outstanding athletes have viewed practice in the same way. Sammy Baugh, for example, the Hall of Fame and former Washington Redskins quarterback, believes that the best way for a young man to develop football ability is to "practice one way. The hard way. If you're a punter, always punt into the wind. If you're an end or halfback and the coach says to run it out 50 yards, run 100. If you're a passer, throw off balance in practice. Don't try to drop back into the pocket in dummy scrimmage and see how accurately you can throw over the top. Throw it sidearm, or off your shoes, or left-handed. The coach knows you can throw it straight overhand, with nobody rushing, or you wouldn't be there. So practice the hard way. Then the games will come easier. Johnny Unitas is the best example of what I mean. Nobody ever outworked him in practice. As a passer, Unitas has the best touch of all."

Tennis champion Rod Laver agrees. "I never loaf, even in practice," he said. "I try to reach every ball. I might have that same kind of play in a crucial game."

When Newell watched Robertson practice defense one day in Rome, he saw that Oscar executed every move perfectly—footwork, balance, darting for the ball. Everything. He asked Robertson where he had learned those fundamentals.

"I did have some coaching, sure," Robertson told Newell. "But it's nothing I've ever given much thought to. I wasn't aware I was doing it fundamentally right. It just felt right."

41

"That," said Newell, "is an example of Oscar's intuitive sense for the game."

Robertson's college coach, George Smith, had a similar experience. In practice one day during Robertson's sophomore season at Cincinnati, Smith watched Robertson drive around his defensive man and drop in a basket.

"Oscar, try that one-and-a-half crossover again," called Smith.

"Say, Coach," asked Robertson, "what do you mean— 'one-and-a-half crossover'?"

Smith laughed. "That's the thing about Oscar," said Smith, later. "He does things other players can't do. Yet he doesn't know he's doin' 'em. That's what they mean by a natural."

Terminology is an elusive thing. Oscar was quite aware of what he was doing, though he had never ascribed a name such as "one-and-a-half crossover" to it. Smith said he had tried to teach the one-and-a-half crossover to his other players for years, but it is a subtle offensive move that can be mastered only through industrious work. "But," added Smith, "the rest of the kids picked it up simply because they saw Oscar doing it so often."

Whether it is true that you can develop basketball techniques by that sort of osmosis is a moot point. It apparently did not work for Arnette. (But it was Wayne Embry who once said, "Oscar made us all better players." So maybe there is something to that after all.)

The backcourt situation shaped up quickly: Robertson, Bockhorn, Smith and Arnette. But who was to start with Robertson? The aging Bockhorn? The compelling but inexperienced Smith? Did rookie Arnette have a chance?

Embry was the center. He had been selected for the NBA

All-Star game for the last three years and was gaining respect around the league, not only as a rugged rebounder but also for his shooting touch—particularly his short jump shot—and for the deftness with which he worked with Robertson, especially the pick-and-roll, where either Robertson would get an easy jump shot or Embry would get a pass from Oscar for a layup.

Lucas was the left forward. The right forward was set with veteran high-scorer Jack Twyman. Boozer and Hawkins competed for top substitute forward.

Training camp is a time of optimism one moment, depression the next. A time of happy hazing when a rookie like Herndon looks all over the locker room for his dazzling new chapeau only to find it sulking slumped and half-drowned in the shower; and a time for hard realities, when someone like skinny Jimmy Rayl, who had been the nation's eighth-leading scorer at Indiana the year before, finds that he must do more than be able to rip off 30-foot jump shots and becomes disheartened and says he has decided to enter graduate school, possibly trying to force the coach's hand. But McMahon says that Rayl has only an outside chance of winning a job and that if he wants to keep trying McMahon will continue to look. Rayl returns to school.

The monotony of training is made up of two-a-day workouts, daily calisthenics, laps around the gym, going over and over the play patterns, fifty free throws before going to the shower, the sweat and strain of scrimmages. There are the three-on-three games, which are as much nostalgia as they are work. It's the schoolyard again. And one day McMahon has three big men, or frontcourtmen, Lucas (6-8), Embry (6-8) and Roberts (6-6) play three small men, or backcourt men, Arnette (6-2), Smith (6-1) and Robertson. A rule that makes the big men groan is that they cannot take the small men under the basket to muscle their points. The premium is on speed, finesse, screens, picks.

There is much good-natured bickering about fouls and what the right score is. The result is a brisk workout for the big men.

"Those little guys," says Lucas afterward, "run right through your legs."

Only a few days left of camp now. Oscar did not play in scrimmage. He had a tooth pulled and sat glumly on the sidelines, jaw cupped in palm. McMahon returned to the barracks where the team stayed and reporters went along. He sprawled on his bunk and shielded his eyes from the brightness in the modest but comfortable barracks. "After this morning's workout," he said, "I need a psychiatrist. The ballhandling was sloppy. We were dull and error-prone." The implication was to the importance of Robertson's presence. "Yes," said McMahon, "they recognize O as the leader."

The talk got around to Lucas, who had shone as his team won 78-68, and he hit 10 of 15 shots and pulled down 14 rebounds. "The optimism all centers around Lucas," said Mc-Mahon. "Other than him, it's the same club that was two games over .500 last year. For years, 57 games has been required to win the division championship. That's a difference of fifteen games for us. I've never seen a player who has changed the thinking of a town so completely as Lucas. That's a lot of pressure on him. But I think he's used to it, and I think he's going to prove to be a great player."

But questions persisted. Lucas still was reluctant to shoot enough. Instead of taking the clear 15- or 18-foot jump shot, he looked to get in closer—but he is not highly adept at penetrating. Lucas was used to working around the basket —starting from there. "And sometimes," said McMahon, evenly, "he gets the opening, goes in and turns his back. This is habit-forming as a pivot man."

On September 25 the Royals held two light workouts, then broke camp. They were to play thirteen exhibition games in fifteen days. In those games, McMahon hoped to find the solution to some of his problems.

6

Amid all the verbal confetti for the coming of Jerry Lucas, Jack Twyman dropped another notch. One rarely read much about Twyman anymore. Newsprint on him began diminishing three years earlier, when Robertson joined the club. Twyman, however, was still one of the most respected men in the NBA, both as an offensive forward and as a gentleman. He took the decline in fan interest stoically.

He is 6-6 (and weighed 215 pounds in 1963) and walks with a forward tilt. The lids of his brown eyes slant at the sides just enough to give him a warm, somewhat quizzical look, and he has a slab jaw at the end of a long face that is ruggedly handsome despite a small mouth that appears to have too many teeth in it.

Once Twyman was the most prominent and popular Royal.

Now, at twenty-nine and going into his ninth pro season, he was the oldest Royal in point of service. Six times he had played in the NBA All-Star game. And now that Dolph Schayes had retired as a player to coach the Philadelphia 76ers (who had just moved from Syracuse and shed the name "Nationals"), only Bob Pettit of St. Louis, among active players, had scored more career points than Twyman. Pettit, a ten-year veteran, had 17,566 points to Twyman's 13,058. That figure also put Twyman fifth on the all-time NBA scoring list.

In 1959, Twyman had averaged 25.8 points a game, second only to Pettit. In 1960 he averaged 31.2 points a game, second to Chamberlain. In 1961 he averaged 22.9 points a game—but then he was second on the *Royals* to Robertson. And the following year he had averaged nearly 20 points a game, eighth in the league.

Most remarkable, though, was Twyman's dedication to the game. He had never missed a regular-season or playoff game. Going into the 1963-64 season he had played in 602 regular-season games, eighteen playoff games and innumerable exhibitions. He was not to miss a preseason game until this season. And through those years, he played with what is almost *de rigueur* in the elbow-strewn, hip-slinging, push-and-tumble life of the NBA: sprained ankles, bruised thighs, blackened eyes and, for a five-week period, a wired jaw.

Twyman also gained the esteem of his colleagues for his efforts with Maurice Stokes. Stokes, the former Royals center, was stricken with encephalitis, a brain injury, after a game in 1958. Twyman accepted guardianship for his immobilized and speechless teammate. Over the years he worked to improve Stokes's spirit and raised more than $100,000 to pay hospital bills. (Much of that money comes from the annual Maurice Stokes Benefit Basketball Game, organized by Twyman and played by NBA stars at Kutsher's

Country Club in the Catskill Mountains.) Even after Stokes died in the early summer of 1970, the benefit game was continued to help the Stokes family.

"I had to take care of Mo," Twyman said. "The rest of the team was leaving town. I was a home-town guy. It was my responsibility. What could I do, just leave Mo alone, penniless, unable to take care of himself? I'm no hero in this thing —in fact, I've been helped by it. Taking care of Mo has made me a better man."

Twyman, of course, did not *have* to take the responsibility. That he did is certainly a reflection of what the man is made of. Also revealing is Twyman's unassuming attitude toward his benevolence. He simply is a man who felt that he could be of help to another man. That's all.

"Mo can talk," Twyman announced to a friend in 1961. He had spent hours at Christ Hospital in Cincinnati trying to get Stokes to move his lips. "You probably couldn't understand him; but he's talking fine."

But Twyman was having his own problems on the court. Never renowned for his defensive work or rebounding, he was a shooter who specialized in the corner jump shot, and he was deadly with it. But now, according to McMahon, the Royals were to emphasize speed. The other forwards had it: Lucas could run some; Hawkins could run; Boozer could run—and Thacker, scheduled to join the team in late fall, could leave a puff of smoke in his wake. Twyman, however, was middle-aged for a ballplayer.

Ever since Wolf took over the club, Twyman had been having difficulties. In Wolf's first year the team lost 12 of 13 games during one early stretch. Wolf, looking for a solution, benched Twyman for two games; in another game, Twyman played less than a half. And it made him angry. "I'd never been treated like that," he said. "I was so mad I couldn't see. I'd come off the bench tense, press my shots, miss easy ones and the home crowd would boo me. Maybe I deserved it, but it made me madder."

There were also rumors that he and Oscar were squabbling for the ball. It was believed that with two shooters like Robertson and Twyman on the same team, there would be the harmony of two hungry foxes for a rabbit. Observers noted that, still early in that first season, Robertson would come downcourt looking for a shot and only upon finding none would he pass off to set up a play.

But, Twyman explained over and over, there was no strain between him and Robertson. "I played with Oz summers when he went to college," said Twyman. "I've always said he was a great player. I don't think there is a backcourtman in the league any better. I'm not his enemy; I'm his admirer. I don't care if he scores 70 every night and I get 10, if we win that way." Another time Twyman said, "Oscar can't miss becoming one of the all-time greats because he's a great student of the game, along with having tremendous natural ability. He has taken over as a leader and he makes us go. He is to us what Bob Cousy is to the Celtics. Everybody knows that he's a great shot, but few know that he can pass with Cousy."

As time went on, Twyman and Robertson worked well together. And by this season, Twyman was Robertson's favorite passing target. Robertson's philosophy is to pass only to someone he is confident can make the shot. "It's silly to give the ball to someone you think will lose it," said Robertson. And Robertson's confidence in Twyman understandably grew.

"Jack is a great jump shooter at all times," said Robertson. "I try to get him the ball if he's open within 15 or 20 feet of the basket, because I feel in my own mind he's going to get it in for us."

Their favorite play was a simple one. The two Royal guards

49

come down the floor. If Robertson is going to free Twyman, he will call the play. Then he passes to the other guard and goes down and picks Twyman's man and the other guard passes to Twyman, who now uses Robertson as a screen to get off his jump shot.

It was true, however, that the two scoring stars did have some trouble adjusting to each other. Said Twyman, "I don't think one man can carry a club, even if he's Pettit or Chamberlain. There's plenty of room for two scorers on a team. Spreading the points takes the pressure off, makes it harder on the defense. That's been one of Boston's secrets for success."

Twyman was playing harder on defense, since he wasn't shooting as much as he had before Robertson's arrival. Once he even volunteered to guard Elgin Baylor. At that time, guarding Baylor was like trying to tame a lion with a twig. Just a few nights before, Baylor had scored 71 points. Against Twyman, Baylor was "held" to 41, while Twyman had 16 and Robertson 17. "They don't want me to score anymore," Twyman said, "so I've got to do something to help." It was the sincere statement of a team man, and his offer to guard Baylor bore that out. But there was also in that statement a trace of bitterness.

Twyman and Robertson had met when Oscar was still in high school. Robertson was visiting the UC campus. George Smith asked alumnus Twyman, then the Royals' No. 1 star, to play a little one-on-one with Robertson.

"George," said Twyman afterward, "if I were you I'd send my wife home and sleep with Oscar tonight. You can't afford to let him out of your sight."

Twyman, Robertson, Embry and Ed Kennedy, Royals' radio announcer, played all-day-long bridge games on the road for years, on buses, on planes, while waiting in airports and bus depots.

"I think," said Twyman, "that you get to know a man that way. I found Oscar to be a very methodical, calculating cardplayer. He thinks about everything, has the whole game mapped out. He knows what he's going to do next. He's a deep thinker, but he'll lead you to believe he's not. He's always thinking, always aware.

"It came out in huddles during games, too. He's really knowledgeable about the game, introspective about it. Instead of saying, 'I'm going to get my 40 points tonight,' he'll think, 'Well, if I can get 28 or 30 I think we can win.' Go down the rosters in the league. How many players can say that they'll do something, and do it?

"But Oz is still pretty much the same guy he was as a freshman at the university. Of course he has matured. But he still has those good attributes, and he is still hard to get to know. He has always stayed to himself."

Though Robertson is usually distant even from his teammates, some still consider him affable and amiable, particularly in the locker room. And, except for Embry, there was no one he enjoyed gibbing more than Bob Boozer. Though Boozer, since losing his starting position to Lucas, was not often in a gay mood, he and Robertson continued to trade friendly barbs.

Robertson would call Boozer "Baby Bob" because of his enthusiasm for skirts, and what fills them. After a game Boozer would dress to kill for a night out. Robertson would warn him, straight-faced, "Don't beat the bushes too late tonight. You need your rest for tomorrow. You don't want Pettit (or Tom Heinsohn or Bailey Howell) to run you into the ground."

And Boozer, rather weakly, would in turn call Robertson "The rolling doughnut," symbolic of the Big O. Boozer may not have fared too well in repartee with Robertson, but he was doing much better on the court. He was easily holding his own against Lucas and would issue complaints—which filtered to the coach and the front office—that at least he should be beaten out of a job on the court, the publicity for Lucas and preseason ticket sales notwithstanding.

"Boozer," said McMahon, "couldn't accept the fact that Lucas could beat him out."

Boozer was 6-8, like Lucas, and, at 225, weighed 5 to 10 pounds less. He had been an All-American at Kansas State and was the Royals' top draft choice in 1959. It was in the NCAA Midwest Regional tournament that Boozer first played against Robertson. This game was, for Boozer, ammunition for his future barbed-word war with Robertson. Whenever he was at a loss, Boozer would bring up this game.

"We used to always get into a hassle about it," said Boozer, smiling. "This is what happened. Oscar was on the free-throw line. I think the score was tied. There were about 10 seconds to go in the game. Well, you know Oscar always takes a lot of time on the free-throw line. He never gets rushed. He likes to get his wind back in those 10 seconds. This time he put the ball down on the line and walked over to say something to his coach. But the referee was counting —you only have 10 seconds to get a free throw off. Oscar rushed back and hurried the shot. And missed. And let me tell you, there were purple-and-white jerseys—Kansas State jerseys—all around that ball when it came off the backboard. Well, we won in double overtime. And Oscar fouled out. He was so mad that he wouldn't sit down. Yeah, we hassle about that a lot."

Boozer played with Oscar on the Pan-Am team in 1959. But, according to Pepper Wilson, something happened to Boozer in the Pan-Am games. "Somehow," said Wilson, "he lost his confidence there."

Boozer did not play with the Royals immediately after Kansas State. He went with the Peoria Caterpillars of the National Industrial Basketball League. Said Wilson, "He began finding himself at Peoria, and then later in the Olympic Games."

It wasn't until the fall of 1960 that Boozer finally played for the Royals. He was often jittery. After starting in some early games, he rode the bench for a while. A mercurial player then—one night he would tear a team apart and the next be torn apart.

Boozer improved rapidly each season, and some NBA observers felt that he was ready to realize his potential to be one of the league's outstanding players. There was never any concern on the club that Boozer was tired from his evenings out. Tom Hawkins, his roommate, said one day, "Boozer slept twelve hours, went down to eat breakfast and then took a nap."

Not only did Boozer lose his starting position, but he had to struggle to be top substitute forward. And the struggle was primarily with, of all people, his roommate.

Hawkins was only 6-5, but it was practically uncontested that he was the best jumping forward from a standing position in the league. He is a beautifully proportioned athlete. With thigh muscles rippling, he runs with a graceful waddle, and when he jumps, he seems to stay aloft so long he looks like a brown suit hanging in a locker.

Hawkins had been a very capable sixth man for the Lakers until being traded to the Royals just before the club opened training camp in September 1962. (A year later the Royals sent forward Hub Reed and cash to Los Angeles in exchange for Hawkins.) Now Hawkins found a niche as top substitute behind forwards Boozer and Twyman.

"Hawkins," McMahon has said, "is just great. A smart, hustling, give-it-all player."

The Royals liked to say he was the second-best sixth man in the league, next to Boston's Frank Ramsey. Los Angeles

Laker fans were wont to say the same. In 1962-63, Hawkins had come off the bench for Cincinnati in the playoffs and hit on 51 percent of his shots and starred on defense, blocking shots and grabbing rebounds. After the Lakers lost to Boston in the NBA championship game, the Cincinnati *Enquirer* reported, "There were howls from LA that with Hawkins they would not have lost 4-2 to the Celtics."

The transition from college ball to the pros had been particularly difficult for Hawkins. An All-American center at Notre Dame, he was the first draft choice of the Lakers (then in Minneapolis) in 1959. He had been a great player at Notre Dame, possibly the best in its history, and was all-city at Chicago's Parker High School.

"When I joined the pros," said Hawkins, "I felt that it would continue that way. I never imagined otherwise."

Hawkins had perfected a turn-around jump shot from the key. It was a simple maneuver. He would get a pass and either take one dribble, twist and jump, or just twist and jump. He had the move so down pat that the ball went from hand to basket as though through a funnel. It was rarely blocked, since it was released with Hawkins, after a characteristic bound, dangling from the rafters.

"I got a rude shock when I arrived at the Lakers' training camp," said Hawkins. "I was getting that turn-around shot stuffed down my throat. 'What is this?' I asked." It seemed that in the pros they deployed some defensive players in the rafters.

"It was also a new experience to learn to shoot with people holding onto your arms and battering you around. Not just some of the time, like in college. But all of the time," said Hawkins. "And then I had to move from the post position to forward. It looked like left field. I knew I would never be a great shooter. I knew that if I was going to stay in the league it would be on hustle and rebounding."

And so Hawkins, who had averaged over 20 points a game at Notre Dame, averaged 9.1 points in his first four years in the pros, though he had occasional big nights, like the 32 points he got against St. Louis in February 1961. But, as it turned out, he stayed in the league for ten years on "hustle and rebounding."

Hawkins was a relatively mediocre shooter from outside, so Robertson helped utilize what offensive strength Hawkins had inside. The two worked a play that was often attempted in the early part of games. It went like this: Robertson passes to Hawkins at the right forward. Then Robertson comes around and Hawkins hands off to him. Now Hawkins is a natural screen and counts 1-2-3. While he is counting the center—usually Embry—slides over and picks Hawkins' defender. At the count of 3, Hawkins races straight down the baseline and Robertson throws a hook pass to Hawkins under the basket.

"I'd say it worked about 80 percent of the time we'd try it," said Hawkins.

Hawkins and Robertson usually got along well. Off the court, Robertson liked to poke fun at Hawkins, as he did Boozer and Embry. Robertson would select one trait and bore in on it. For Boozer it was ladies. For Embry it was his casual concern for details (known, to Oscar, as sloppiness). For Hawkins it was his smoothness. Hawkins is as flowing off the court as he is on. Hawkins can be persuasive, a charmer, disarmingly cordial. He has done public-relations work in the off-season, as well as television and radio work in the Los Angeles area. His face has a gentle openness despite brows that almost meet (similar in this respect to Lucas) and almost give a churlish impression. There is a gap in his teeth that is quickly forgotten because of a voice so mellifluous it seems studied. With a broad smile, Hawkins would bear the brunt of a good-natured attack on his urbanity and good looks by Robertson. According to Hawkins, Robertson is "a perfectionist on the court and he expects that same kind of perfection from you. And he lets you know how he feels. It could rankle. Oscar can really get angry if you blow an assist. He doesn't forget easily. And if it costs a game, you know that he is thinking unflattering thoughts about you. As any great person, though, he is temperamental. Look at Ted Williams. Or Maria Callas."

(Newell has a similar view: "I have never seen a talented person who wasn't temperamental.")

Even Embry said, "I still feel as though I don't really know Oscar. And I roomed with him for six years."

Embry was an easy and obvious foil for Robertson. At 6-8, 250, he was just this side of elephantine. At first glance he appears so mammoth that one is surprised when he actually moves. But Embry worked hard, in games and in practice. He was an unselfish player with a forceful drive to win. A menacing rebounder, he still kept a cool head on the court. And some of the players around the league referred to him as "The Enforcer" because of his singular ability to restore law and order when an altercation broke out. Said one player, "When he shakes his finger under your nose and says, 'Calm down,' you'd better calm down. That finger's like a blackjack."

His hands are exceptionally large, so he was nicknamed "Goose" after "Goose" Tatum of the Harlem Globetrotters, who also had large hands. When he was at Miami University in Oxford, Ohio, Embry worked in the cafeteria of a dormitory for part of his scholarship money. Bob Kurz, who later became the school's sports-publicity director, worked with Embry and recalls, "We all took turns washing dishes, but Wayne amazed us. He could actually pick up three dishes simultaneously, spread them out like a fellow playing a game of cards and wash them that way."

Embry began making his mark in basketball at Tecumseh High School in New Carlisle, Ohio. In his senior year he made the all-Ohio second team. Second team was not exactly a disgrace, however. Accompanying Embry was a player from Tiltonville who later became a baseball player with the Pittsburg Pirates, Bill Mazeroski, and a player from Columbus South High who also chose baseball as a profession, Frank Howard.

At Miami of Ohio, Embry developed an accurate hook shot and became a star. That one shot, along with muscle under the boards, was about as much offensive artillery as he needed in college. The pros were different, though. It was necessary for him to develop an effective short jump shot, for two reasons. First, as just another weapon, obviously. But second, it would make it more difficult to defense Robertson.

When Oscar drove he needed the lane clear, and Embry's standing under the basket would be as helpful as a roadblock. So Embry had to move out, and when he did he was often left open, since his man then tried to help stop Oscar. And Robertson, always aware of the open man, could whip a pass to Embry.

The 10-foot shot was something new for Embry, so he stayed after practice jump-shooting, jump-shooting, jump-shooting to perfect it. "I had to do it, I had to adjust," said Embry. "And I knew I would get the ball from him some way, bounce pass, hook pass, flip."

("Wayne," said Dick Shrider, Miami's coach, "would make whatever sacrifices he had to make to succeed.")

Embry was probably the shortest center in the NBA, and one of the widest. But, many Royals' critics moaned that the Royals did not have the "big man" necessary to win.

"What do they mean 'big man'?" McMahon wanted to know in training camp. "Embry is 6 feet 8 and weighs 250 pounds. He has a hand span that is about the length of a foot ruler, fingertip to fingertip. Those big men—those tall men—didn't do so well last year, with the exception of Russell. Chamberlain and Bellamy didn't even get their teams in the playoff. Embry is big where it counts most—in the heart."

Embry was popular with the players and was the team captain for the three years Wolf was there. He had the respect of the players because of his desire and endurance, and he had the love of the players because of his even temper. He also had some of the endearing qualities of Winnie the Pooh, who somehow always had jam on his face and never knew it.

Embry's first NBA game was memorable for a lapse that could be excused only because of his unbridled enthusiasm. When the Royals departed from the Cincinnati airport and flew to Minneapolis to play the Lakers, Embry was thrilled and had visions of becoming Cincinnati's answer to George Mikan. There was just one problem when the team arrived at the Minneapolis arena. While all the other players in the locker room dug their hands into their duffel bags, Embry dug his hands into his pockets. In his excitement he had left all his gear in a friend's car at the Cincinnati airport. Something had to be done.

Embry played, and there were applause and chuckles as the rookie came onto the court. He had obtained one of the Lakers' road uniforms and turned the pants and shirt inside out. He was a spectacle, but he was playing. And by his third season he had played himself into an All-Star berth.

But if Embry and Oscar worked well together on the court, it was not always that way in their room. Robertson watches television with a mania, anything from quiz shows to late-morning soap operas where people are always fainting. "And," said Embry, "late, late, late, late movies that he's seen fifteen times. He watches until it goes off. And he can't understand when I don't want to watch. Hell, I want to sleep. Is that so hard to understand?"

After a game, Oscar would be propped on his bed, a beer and sandwhich in his hands, the rays of the television flickering over his body, and he would watch, watch, watch. In the other bed, Embry, a weary but restless whale, tossed and turned under his sea of blankets.

There were moments, adds Embry, when the television was not on and the two often talked basketball. "He has made a science of the game," said Embry. "He is my idea of a real man. Intelligent, driving, knows what he wants and how to get it. He came from a poor neighborhood—like we all did, and he had it rough. He would do everything he could to improve his game. Why, sometimes we'd just be sitting around the room and he would have a ball and practice fingertip control on shooting."

Robertson and Embry enjoyed other topics of discussion, too. In casual conversation with Embry after his retirement from basketball in 1969, he was asked what else he and Robertson talked about when they roomed together. Embry adjusted his horn-rimmed glasses that he wears in public— and which were rather befitting the important office he fills (probably literally, too) as head of the recreation department for the City of Boston—and said with a grin, "What do men usually talk about?"

Now as the Royals were preparing their exhibition schedule, Embry, like the rest of the players, was optimistic. There was relative harmony in the club, though a professional team, like any other business or even household, cannot be free of dissident aspects. Embry—like Boozer, Hawkins, Smith and Robertson—was reaching his peak. Only Bockhorn and Twyman were on the dark side of the calendar. Arnette was a superior rookie prospect with agility and poise and unequaled speed. But it was Lucas whom they all looked to for the extra push, in scoring and in rebounding, to send them over the top as world champions.

"We have," Embry said, "the best team in the NBA. And we have the best player in the NBA, Oscar. We will win."

It was a pretty good possibility, but it was still six months too soon to say.

7

Thirteen games in fifteen days. It was the exhibition season, but it was a taste of the months ahead—the jostling bus in the dark, the players wearily watching the flick of unending streetlights click by; the airplanes to catch at eight in the morning after a restless night following a tough game; bones creaking like old hinges; tender palms, even the duffel bag raising callouses.

To another town (Where? Which one? They overlap in memory), to another game (with more elbows and pushing and straining and a crash to the floor that sends bolts of pain in the ankle), before more crowds (so many gleaming teeth and jackhammer voices). But also the exultation of good play: a stolen pass in a crucial moment; an effective fake and a quick jump shot that pops the net while your defensive man is tumbling backward. And the court, with the bright lights illuminating it. You are center of attraction. They have all come to see you perform. And then a victory. Somehow it lifts the spirit. After all, that's what you're after. To practice, to struggle, to sacrifice to be the best. For the heart, but for the wallet, too. More points for me, more wins for the team, more money for everyone. Score. Score. Score. Win. Win. Win.

There was a difference, though, in the exhibition schedule. There were no Chicagos or New Yorks or San Franciscos to travel to. For the Royals, there were towns like Fort Dodge, Iowa; Huntingburg, Indiana; Chillicothe, Ohio. The high school gymnasium is packed with people who will get this one chance to see the greatest basketball players in the world in person—and *the* greatest basketball player, The Big O.

The games do not count in the standings, but they do count. They count at the box office, where the admissions help pay training expenses. And what the coach observes on the court adds up in his mind. Now, for the first time, McMahon's Royals would perform against NBA competition. Where did the team need to be honed? And as always: How Will Lucas Do?

His debut was delayed. The Royals had broken camp on September 25, gone to Cincinnati and then flown to Galesburg, Illinois, for their first exhibition game, against the St. Louis Hawks. Lucas had come down with strep throat and watched from the bench.

The Royals had several exhibition games scheduled with the Hawks. The Hawks—with a front line of Pettit, Cliff Hagan and Zelmo Beaty, and guards Richie Guerin and Lennie Wilkens—were one of the powers of the league and had finished second to the Lakers in the Western Division the year before.

Lucas would be tested by All-Star veteran Bob Pettit, at that time the leading scorer in the history of the NBA. A tough, aggressive, persistent forward, Pettit, balding now, was the man who could teach a rookie what the game was about. And the lesson was a bruising one, for the abdomen as well as the ego.

Lucas watched Pettit score 29 points in the first game as the Hawks won a close one, 119-113.

The Royals had led by 4 points in the fourth quarter. Then Wilkens hit on two straight baskets and the score was tied, 107-107. He hit three more in a row and the Royals could only hustle to keep the score close.

Robertson started the year well. He was the Royals' high-point man with 27 points and made 13 of 15 free throws.

After the game, McMahon said, "They were getting a lot of second efforts." The allusion was to the value of Lucas the rebounder. With Luke in the lineup, Pettit, Hagan and Beaty would not have dominated the boards. As for Robertson, McMahon said succinctly, "As good as ever."

Lucas was in the lineup the next day, at Rockford, Illinois. It was, he told himself as he suited up in the locker room, just an exhibition game. There was nothing to be tense about. How many times had he faced pressure games? The state tournaments in high school, the NCAA championships with Ohio State. It was just another game. Or was it?

The Royals got the opening tipoff, and as Lucas came downcourt he found Pettit guarding him. He also felt a shove with a chest. He was being guarded tightly. Robertson had the ball and looked to Lucas, but Lucas was now swathed in the arms of Pettit, so the ball had to be worked to Twyman's side.

As the game progressed, Lucas seemed a bit bewildered. He would come down on offense, two right fingertips habitually going to the mouth for a quick lick, and then be met by the all-encompassing Pettit.

Lucas was never a mobile player. "I'm not a great one-on-one player," he has said. "And I've never been good with the ball, so there's never been any sense clearing out a side for me." He would need a pick or screen. Or a pass into the pivot as he cut through. Or score on a tip or rebound. But it was hard going. Pettit gave him no room to maneuver.

On defense, it was much the same. Pettit used his elbows, his hips, his fakes, his strength—in short, his experience to demoralize Lucas. In that first game, though, Lucas scored 13 points, making five field goals. But the Hawks won again, 106-104.

The next night both clubs traveled to Memphis. This time the Royals won, 93-90, their first victory of the season. Again Lucas got a going-over by Pettit, but he was improving. McMahon gave him credit for doing a good defensive job on Pettit in the first half, holding him to 8 points. But Lucas was learning another lesson. In the NBA the first half often bears little resemblance to the second. Lucas scored 16 and Oscar 20 in the game. Bud Olsen was praised for hitting some key second-quarter baskets in place of Embry.

"Basically," said Lucas, "I'm a neophyte. I've got a lot to learn. I'm just finding my way."

After a day off the Hawks and Royals moved on to Nashville, where the Hawks won their third, 105-97. Smith had been starting at guard, but tonight Bockhorn was in at the opening tipoff. He made just one field goal and four free throws. The Royals were outplayed and outfought throughout.

McMahon, who is known as a "sufferer" on the bench,

grimaced and grunted and rolled his eyes at the roofbeams as the Royals committed turnovers, came in second on loose balls and were often shut out under the boards. The team was still feeling its way, groping.

In four games, Pettit had scored 91 points, mostly off Lucas, while Lucas had just 39.

"Jerry's going through what I did when I came out of Louisiana State," said Pettit. "I played center in college with my back to the basket and when I came into the NBA I had to change my entire game. Once he adjusts he'll be fine."

Periodically, McMahon would take Embry out, send Lucas into the pivot and send Boozer or Hawkins into the left-forward spot. It was a move designed to restore Lucas' confidence by putting him in familiar surroundings.

"The hardest transition," said Lucas, "was moving from center to forward. I was happy to get back once in a while. It settled me down."

McMahon also envisioned Lucas playing defense against the best centers in the league. "He doesn't commit himself real quick," said McMahon. "He won't be faked out easily. And I don't feel Russell will be too strong for him. I have no qualms about putting Jerry on defense against Russell."

But it was at forward where Lucas had to make it. As long ago as rookie camp, McMahon saw that Lucas could shoot from outside. "He's shown me he can work out of the corner," said McMahon, "and he's shown me a good outside shot. If he can hit it consistently, they have to play him tight and make it easier for him to go to the offensive boards."

Robertson and Lucas also had a period of adjustment (which would continue throughout their careers). Lucas had to adjust to Robertson's game. It would not be the reverse. Robertson plays a game of action, there is constant movement, regardless of whether you have the ball. If you stand as stuck as a fire hydrant, you get nothing. But break once, get just a nip of daylight, and you have a perfect lead pass from Robertson.

Lucas was learning, sometimes with chagrin, sometimes with a flush of anger, that Robertson runs the show. "At times," he said with restraint, "it was a problem."

In high school and in college the offense had revolved around Lucas. Now he had to look to someone else for leadership. Oscar, though, was helpful in his way, for he wanted to win.

Lucas saw that Robertson was trying to put him on the right track. "Oscar," Lucas would admit much later, "was a great help. He set up the plays and he ran the club. But then, who was more qualified to run it than him?"

Despite differences in personality and in their approach to the game, Lucas would always say, "To me, he is The Best, in two quick words. He does so many things so well. He's got the ball on a rubberband, he doesn't even have to look at it. You can't stop him. And he's a great competitor."

But still they weren't clicking. Nor was the team. The Hawks and Royals were now in Quincy, Illinois, and at the half the Royals were losing, 53-45. The play was ragged. McMahon, his Irish face reddened with rage, burst into the locker room and spit out a stream of invective. The players were sullen, too, and Robertson was angry. He had not started the game because of a cold in his back. Heat treatments eased the tightness, but at the half he had only 7 points.

For even Oscar has nights when nothing falls for him. "Sometimes," Oscar said, "I get to feeling nothing I throw up will drop in. All I can do then is set up the other guys. Then maybe I hit a shot and I feel hot again."

Lucas came out and played the third quarter as though his future depended on it. He rebounded and ran and scored

9 of the team's 34 points in the third quarter. Oscar, too, found the range and finished with 20 points. Lucas had 18.

"Lucas," said McMahon afterward, "looked better in all respects than in his previous four games."

It was the first time since training camp that the Royals had looked good, the first time they showed the promise of championship caliber. It was noteworthy to both the Royals in general and Robertson in particular that the Royal's best night so far was also Lucas' best night so far.

On to Fort Dodge the next day, and again the tough Hawks. The Royals, though improving, still could not muster enough to beat the Hawks. They lost again, by 2 points, 109-107. Robertson had 22 points, Lucas only 12.

Two days later at Chillicothe, things began looking up, in some respects. The Royals did win, beating the New York Knicks, 116-112. It was a close game, too close, since it was against the weak Knicks (last place last year and little hopes of climbing any higher this year). The team was composed of players who are known on the sports pages as "journeymen"; "players who do yeomen work" is another description. But for the rough fans at Madison Square Garden they were "nothin' but a bunch of bums." They included Dave Budd, Tom Hoover, Gene Conley, Art Heyman, Bob Nordmann and John Rudometkin. Tom Gola and Johnny Green were two players who would stick around quite a while in the NBA. There was also Paul Hogue, who had played at the University of Cincinnati and might have been recruited by the mystique of having gone to the same school as Oscar Robertson. They had played together one year.

Robertson crashed through with a drive shot with 3:54 left in the game. It broke the tie. The win was the Royal's third in seven games. Not an imposing record.

October 5. A day Lucas will never forget. The Fairgrounds fieldhouse in Columbus was jammed with people who wanted to watch Jerry Lucas as a pro. They were the same people who had jammed the Ohio State gym for four years to watch Lucas the Buckeye. When Lucas came out onto the court he received a ten-minute standing ovation.

"And then," said Jack McMahon, "Luke proceeded to play the worst game you ever saw."

The Knicks won, 117-102. Lucas scored 9 points, 7 in the first half. He made two free throws in the second. He made just 3-out-of-12 field-goal attempts for the game. In contrast, Robertson was beginning to put his game together. He had 26 points, with 9 of 14 from the floor, and had 7 assists and 4 rebounds.

For Lucas the game was humbling from a physical standpoint, too. McMahon had him at center some of the game. He was up against Hogue, who was 6-9, 240, and Nordmann, 6-10, 250. Sometimes one-against-one, sometimes they were both in against him. The infighting was vicious and Lucas did not get the best of it. After the game he was disconsolate in the locker room. His white Royal uniform with the red-and-blue stripe down the left-front side was wet with perspiration.

"I don't know," said Lucas. "Sure it was tough. But the thing is, I have never shot so badly."

McMahon, looking for any bright spot, said, "If there was a hopeful sign, it was that Luke looked better at forward than he did in the pivot."

Jim Schottelkotte, covering the Royals for the Cincinnati *Enquirer,* did not comment on Lucas in the pivot; he did, however note his work at his new position: "Lucas is still obviously lost at forward."

McMahon mentioned something else. He said that Lucas was just not looking for his shots right now. "It's no problem," he assured. But it *was* a problem, and McMahon knew it. Lucas was only attempting the shot he seemed certain to make. He was taking few risks, thus immobilizing himself even further on offense. McMahon wanted him to work harder for shots, to get in the game more. In short, shoot more.

After a while, the team discovered why Lucas was not shooting more. Lucas took great pride in his field-goal percentage. At Ohio State he had led the nation three straight years in shooting percentage with the stupendous figures of .637, .623, .611. According to several players, Lucas tallied his shooting statistics in his head. An unwritten basketball law says that such work is the province of the scorekeeper. The theory being that while in hot pursuit of victory it is the team that is of sole importance. But, except for rare instances, this is not true in professional sports. A professional is one who plays for money. Of course he wants the team to win— more money (and inner satisfaction is an added plus)—but if he does not have an impressive portfolio of statistics at contract time, his wallet will be measurably lighter than one belonging to a teammate who has more palpable evidence of his achievements. The tallying of scoring statistics during a game is accomplished with much hugger-mugger. To reveal such a thing is gauche in the extreme. And when the players found out, it did nothing to raise their esteem of Lucas. It was understandable that McMahon and the rest of the Royals wanted Lucas to shoot more—even at the cost of finishing with a lower field-goal percentage— and to catch up on his statistical reading with the rest of them: in the postgame sheets distributed in the locker room.

After the Knicks' game there was more unfavorable news. It was learned that Tom Thacker would not get his release from the Army until December. The Royals had been hoping to have him on the club by the end of October.

On the road again, next day, Terre Haute: This time the Royals beat New York, 130-120. Robertson played his best game of the exhibition season, scoring 31 points. The next day, Lafayette, in the Purdue Fieldhouse, the Baltimore Bullets this time: the Royals won big, 132-97. Embry had 25 points, Oscar, 18, Luke, 14.

The next day, Lafayette again, the Bullets again: The Royals lost, 97-95. But something happened that night. The emergence of Jerry Lucas. He scored 23 points and pulled down 20 rebounds, and afterward McMahon said he was absolutely great.

It was an impressive showing, since the Bullets were amply fortified on the front line: Walt Bellamy, 6-11, 225, Gus Johnson, 6-6, 235, Bill McGill, 6-9, 225, and Terry Dischinger, 6-7, 190. Only a fourth-place team in the Western Division last year, but the team was young and seemed to be improving.

The two clubs traveled to Huntingburg, Indiana, for a game the next night. Two thousand fans were tucked into the local high school gym. The Royals battered the Bullets, 142-106. Lucas dominated the backboards. There are times when Walt Bellamy is as formidable as a sleepwalker, and this night was one of them. It is always a question whether his drowsiness is self-inducing or stimulated by outside sources—for example, the discouragment of a fiery Jerry Lucas.

McMahon, still looking for a second starting guard, saw Bockhorn and Smith score 16 each. Arnette had 13, and McMahon made it official that Arnette would stick with the club. "His blinding speed makes our club click," he said. "Jay has started three games, and those were the games we looked the best in."

McMahon was also pleased with Robertson. A coach must get along with his star player if he is to get along with anyone. He found Oscar to be receptive to new ideas on the court, particularly his (McMahon's) ideas. "Oscar has cooperated in every way to try to get my patterns across," said McMahon. "I'm a new coach with a different style—mine happens to be more of a running game—someone else might not have taken to it so readily." McMahon also noted that Oscar had been shooting "fabulously." The next evening, Oscar bore him out, scoring 25 points in the Royals' 117-113 win over Baltimore.

The Royals won their last game of the exhibition season, and it gave them a winning record, 7 victories, 6 losses.

Though there had been lapses that sent McMahon into deep gloom, there was still much to elicit optimism. Oscar was playing with his usual skill and aplomb. Lucas, despite low points expected of a rookie but not a superman, was going to be a fine asset: He could shoot inside and outside, he could rebound, he could pass. Embry's short jump shot could now be depended on and he was a solid rebounder. Twyman, according to McMahon, was still a great shooter. Though he was ailing some this exhibition season, missing the first game of his career, Twyman was still shooting well. He was not the consistently superb outside shooter he had been, but expectations were high for him.

Bockhorn's stability, Smith's shooting, Arnette's speed, made the second starting-guard spot a pleasant problem for McMahon. He would not decide on the starter until the night of the first regular-season game. The top front-line reserves, Boozer and Hawkins, would start on other clubs. Olsen, who would be in to relieve Embry, was still an unknown quantity but had shown ability in the exhibition games. He was a surprisingly good passer from the pivot as well as a sturdy rebounder though not much of a scorer.

After the final exhibition game, Mack Herndon and Joe Roberts were cut. Herndon was never to play in the NBA. Roberts—who had spent three mediocre years with the then-Syracuse Nationals—was returned to the Philadelphia 76ers. He had been with Cincinnati on trial loan. If he had made the club, the Royals would have reimbursed Philadelphia. Roberts never again played in the NBA. Neither cut was surprising. Another expected occurrence that day, October 11: Embry was named captain again.

The Royals would open the season October 16 against the Hawks at St. Louis. Then they would fly home and confront the world-champion Boston Celtics the following evening. On Monday, October 14, the Royals held their final practice. Lucas sat it out, said his knees were bothering him. Otherwise the team was physically fit and looked snappy in drills. There was a lightness to the team, a confidence, a curiosity. Some national magazines picked them to take the championship from the Celtics. Oscar thought they were very good.

"I feel right now," said McMahon, "that we have a good enough club to win it all."

8

Robertson has contended that to win championships it takes more than one man, whether he be a great backcourtman or a hulking center. It takes a total effort from the administration on down. And the administration of the Royals, Robertson has felt, has always been lackluster.

The problems of club ownership persisted. As the team went through training camp and exhibition games, there were rumors about the sale of the club to Warren Hensel, then a minority stockholder. Hensel was trying to complete a deal to buy the Royals from Emprise Corporation of Buffalo, New York, which had recently purchased controlling interest from the Thomas E. Wood estate of Cincinnati. Lou Jacobs owned Sports Service, a $50-million concessions empire that sells food and beverages in arenas, airports and shopping centers in the United States and Europe. One of its arms was Emprise. Hensel announced that he and Emprise had agreed for him to purchase 56 percent, or "control," of the stock.

It seemed there was some minor difficulty over the leasing of Cincinnati Gardens. But on September 27, the day of the first exhibition game, it was announced that Emprise had paid $400,000 for 40 percent of the Gardens and had retained 56 percent of the club. Hensel was obviously out. Ambrose Lindhorst, counsel for Jacobs, said that negotiations with Hensel had terminated after six months. Hensel said there had been an agreement in writing, which the Jacobs people were not honoring. Lindhorst said that the claim had no foundation.

The reason behind the Jacobs move was that they apparently believed the Royals, with Robertson and Lucas, would not only be contenders for years to come but good box office as well. The bulk of the Royals stock was turned over to Lou Jacobs' 27-year-old son Jerry. Later, in February, it would be revealed that Hensel owned only 1/186 of the Royals. This came as a surprise to a lot of people, including Odie Smith and Charley Wolf, who thought they were being criticized by someone with greater financial influence than that.

The front office continued to lack stability and purpose, which affected the team in a distasteful, if only indirect, way. And Oscar, hoping for a smooth organization to pave the way to a championship, was disenchanted. In years to come, when asked why the Royals were not champions, Robertson would redirect the question: "I am the wrong man to ask about why we haven't won a title. You should be asking our front office."

Robertson considered it folly, for example, to have traded people like Clyde Lovellette in 1958, and later Boozer and

Embry, and to have allowed Dick Ricketts to quit basketball to enter the St. Louis Cardinals' farm system as a pitcher. In 1967 the Royals would be one of the first NBA teams to lose a first-round draft choice, Mel Daniels, to the new American Basketball Association. Also in that year, they would fail to sign their third-round draft choice, Sam Smith, who, like Daniels, signed with the Minneapolis club of the ABA. In the search for a big man, Robertson feels the Royals could have drafted Willis Reed—now an All-Star with the Knicks —but out of sheer incompetence (and possibly racial considerations) failed to do so.

Another gripe was that the Royals fell down in the promotion department. "They don't advertise on radio or television," said Robertson. "I have friends who ask me, 'Hey, when's your next game?' and we're playing that night. The whole league is like that." Said Oscar another time, "The franchise is now much better than it was at the beginning. But it still has a long way to go. The league as a whole has a long way to go. The league is not improving as much as the caliber of the ballplayers."

He has been incensed at his salary negotiations as much as anything else concerning the Royals. Virtually every year there has been a contretemps concerning his salary. When he has not been an actual holdout, then he has threatened to hold out. One year, Robertson did not report to camp and did not look like he was going to, so the Royals began making feelers around the league to obtain another guard.

"I'm a professional," he said before the 1967 season. "I've been indoctrinated. I play for money and I'm going to get what I think I'm worth. If the money is not there, I will not play. It's the same old story. I've been here for seven years and I've been producing for seven years."

What Robertson desired is much like what the Red Sox were reported to have done with Ted Williams and the

Yankees with Mickey Mantle: send the star a contract with
the money line left blank. The star fills it in. The maneuver
seems foolhardy and was probably the pipedream of some
imaginative sportswriter. But the essence of the tale is that
the club appreciated their star so much they said, "Here, we
give you the world."

"I don't look for this kind of trouble at contract time,"
Robertson said. "Yet I always have trouble. I know I have
been paid more each time, but it never comes easy."

Pepper Wilson always told him about the "economics of
Cincinnati." That is, the club just could not afford to pay
Robertson the kind of figures he demanded because, as Wilson said, "It's a little Dutch town. We've got Proctor and
Gamble here, we wash the nation and brush the people's
teeth. We've got the mills. They help keep the economy
steady. But it's a conservative town, in terms of money."

Wilson also noted that 60 percent of the Royals' attendance comes from out-of-town fans, from Kentucky, Indiana and West Virginia, and from other parts of Ohio, em-
phasizing that Cincinnati itself has difficulty supporting professional sports. The Royals' tickets of $4 tops was, along
with Baltimore's, the least expensive in the league. Yet complaints were common among fans that prices were too high.
And after 1964, the games would no longer be on radio at
all and the Royals would play a third of their home games in
Cleveland and Omaha.

Other teams besides the Royals have felt the bite of the
populace there. The Reds have often struggled along with
some of the poorest attendance figures in the major leagues.
A good minor-league hockey team folded in the mid-Sixties.
Cincinnati and Xavier, the two prominent college football
teams in town, are not very successful at the turnstile. The
Cincinnati Bengals, an AFL expansion team, caught on, but
not immediately. Playing at Nippert Stadium, the U of C's

football home, the Bengals under Paul Brown had trouble filling a relatively small stadium with a seating capacity of 28,000.

"It's a funny thing," said Wilson. "The original prophet without honor could have settled here. The best thing that ever happened to the Bengals was that they were not granted local ownership. Paul Brown's name is now selling that team. An outsider. The people here have a tendency to look down on their own kind, their own people."

In the beginning, of course, the Royals were outsiders. They had been in Rochester from the time of the National Basketball League in 1945, the Basketball Association of America in 1948, the National Professional Basketball League in 1949 and finally the NBA in 1950. From their beginning in 1945, the Rochester Royals did not have a losing season until 1954. They were league champions twice. Despite success with their opponents, the Royals had less luck with their accounting department. The team never made much money. And it began to lose money regularly during the 1954-55, 1955-56 and 1956-57 seasons, when it was a less-than-.500 team in the standings for the first time in its history.

Owners Les and Jack Harrison sought to move the club, and Cincinnati seemed an ideal spot. The NBA's territorial draft arrangement made Cincinnati an appealing spot for a pro-basketball team. The local college had a hot-shot sophomore named Robertson, and as one writer put it, "It is necessary to realize that this is a basketball team that existed—strategically, emotionally and financially—for the Coming of The Big O."

A local Cincinnati syndicate tried to dig up enough money to buy the club from the Harrisons, fell short, then went to Tom Wood, a real-estate and insurance mogul in town. Purchase price of the club was $250,000. The syndicate still needed $200,000. Wood, a sportsman, tossed in the required amount and the club came to Cincinnati in 1957, then sat around twiddling with their empty wallets until Robertson arrived on the scene in 1960.

Actually, Robertson was on the scene, but to the detriment (at that time) of the pros. Cincinnati was agog over Robertson. Pepper Wilson had said that people in Cincinnati did not know a basketball was round until Oscar landed on the UC campus. In the three seasons before Oscar played varsity ball for the Bearcats, they had a 52-22 record and had drawn 185,244 fans at home (and 377,007 overall). At the same time the Royals were languishing both in the standings and in the financial ledgers. But the owners were like traffic cops behind a billboard: They were waiting for Robertson to hit the road.

During Robertson's junior and senior years at UC, the Royals finished last (winning but nineteen games each season) and lost over $150,000. The show was at the other end of town and the people of this "Dutch town" were saving their nickels for Robertson. So the Royals waited and did not expend much energy on promotion and other such fripperies.

"They did a sensible thing," said Eddie Gottlieb, then owner of the Philadelphia Warriors. "The Royals people kept their losses to a minimum until Oscar finished school, then they had a chance to wipe out the red ink."

In Robertson's senior year with the Bearcats the Royals were already capitalizing on Robertson for the coming season, though rumors that he was considering joining the Harlem Globetrotters were dismissed rather briefly. By June of 1960 the Royals were $40,000 ahead of the previous season in advance-ticket sales. For the first time they were not just surviving in Cincinnati but seemed to be prospering.

But there were to be some restive nights for the Royal owners before Robertson was a signed member of the squad

—and those nights were an indication of the tough Robertson line on money. Abe Saperstein, owner of the Harlem Globetrotters, was loathe to concede Robertson to the Royals. Two years before, Saperstein had enticed Wilt Chamberlain to relinquish his college career at the University of Kansas for what may or may not have been a more lucrative position with the Globetrotters.

Robertson considered the offer, though it is doubtful that he would have played for the clowning Globetrotters over the straight NBA. Robertson has too much pride in his basketball talents to allow them to be squandered as a comedic heavy—his assertion that he is a *professional* basketball player who plays for pay notwithstanding. This was not Robertson's first offer by the Globetrotters. He had been approached the year before, at the end of his junior year. Saperstein was willing to pay him $60,000 a year to bounce around the world with his group of entertainers. Robertson went to Jake Brown for advice.

"It was really a tempting offer," said Brown, "especially since Oscar was having a lot of family problems at the time. His mother needed a kidney operation, the home in Indianapolis was badly in need of repairs and, to top it off, his mother had fallen victim to an unscrupulous subcontractor."

But Brown advised Robertson to borrow enough money from a bank to alleviate the financial problems of the moment, saying that Robertson's basketball future was sufficient collateral.

"Stick it out," said Brown, "and earn your degree. In the long run, it'll mean more to you than Saperstein's offer."

Robertson went home, slept on it and informed Saperstein that he would remain a student.

"How many other kids would have refused the offer?" asked Brown. "Wilt Chamberlain didn't. Oscar has a lot of character and a lot of pride and a deep loyalty to the University of Cincinnati."

Now though, Robertson was using the Globetrotters as a lever to pry more money from the Royals. Finally, on September 10, Robertson signed a three-year contract with the Royals for $100,000. An off-season job with Tom Wood's insurance company was added for topping.

"No rookie but Wilt Chamberlain ever received more," said one person close to the scene.

But no man is indispensable, as the saying goes. And the Royal owners, in moments of reflection, had to consider what action to take if Robertson did in fact take flight with the Globetrotters.

"The team would have stayed one more year in Cincinnati," said a Royal executive, "but if it didn't draw—and there was no reason why it should—the franchise would have been unloaded in 1961."

But Robertson came. The Royals stayed. Fans streamed to Cincinnati Gardens.

The season before, Royals' attendance was 58,244. With the rookie Robertson the Royals passed the 1959-60 figure in a little less than a fourth of the season. By the middle of January the Royals had twice drawn over 10,000 fans to games and the single-game club record was set on New Year's Day 1961, when 10,289 paid to see the Royals beat St. Louis 114-112. Five days later a crowd of 9,461 watched Robertson and the Royals play the Celtics. And this night was significant. For nearby, for the first time that season, the University of Cincinnati basketball team was playing at home. The Bearcats played Houston and won in overtime. But their attendance was only 5,290.

Another occurrence of note took place on January 19, less than three weeks after the record-breaking crowd. The Royals drew only 2,481 while losing to the Knicks. The reason was not that the Knicks were the last-place team in the Eastern Division; nor that the Royals had lost 6 out of their last 7. The reason was the pregame announcement that Oscar Robertson, who had suffered a bruised hip in a game the night before, would not suit up for the Knick game.

The Royals went on to draw a total of 194,017 in 31 home games in Robertson's first season for an average of 6,258 per game. That was more than the entire home attendance for the previous *three* years the Royals had been in Cincinnati—three years without Robertson.

One thing still plagued the "new" Royals. They did not make the playoffs. In the two seasons before Robertson the Royals finished last in the Western Division. With Robertson they did it again, though with a bit more style. They finished one game behind the third-place Detroit Pistons, with a 33-46 record. The Pistons were 34-45. In the two previous years they had concluded their dreary ways nine games to the rear of Detroit and six behind Minneapolis, respectively.

Though the Royals rose in the standings the next two seasons—finishing second in 1961-62 and third in 1962-63—attendance slowly decreased until a new legend incarnate, Jerry Lucas, arrived. The Royals had drawn 146,468 for 31 home games in 1961-62 and 137,739 for 33 home games in 1962-63.

But as advance sales showed, Cincinnatians were about to flood the gates of the Gardens once again. Fans were already lining up, in spirit if not in fact, for the home opener of the 1963-64 season with the Celtics.

9

Your average lion's pit cannot contain 8,816 creatures. Except for that minor point, Kiel Auditorium in St. Louis measured up in most respects. NBA players who came to contest the Hawks were made immediately aware of this. The fans were considered the most vociferous in the league. In addition, there were twenty special seats reaching almost to the playing floor and known as "Murderers' Row" for the habitués there who customarily hurled oaths like rocks. On occasion, rival teams even worked plays where a pass would hopefully find its way into the mouth of one of those fans.

The tough Hawks took up on the court where the fans left off in the stands. It was some place to begin a season, some place to begin a career. But the Royals and Robertson and Lucas were up to the challenge. The Royals won, 112-93. Robertson—"with his usual magnificent heroics," read the morning paper's account—scored 22 points. He fed off for fifteen more baskets and in so doing tied the auditorium record. Embry was high scorer for the evening with 25. McMahon had settled on Smith as his other starting guard, and it was a happy decision. Smith scored 13 points. But the night belonged to Jerry Lucas—with some reservations.

Lucas played 44 of the 48 minutes, scored 23 points on 9 buckets in 14 attempts and 5 free throws out of 6 and had 17 rebounds. Lucas's unremitting counterpart, Pettit, scored 39 points, however. "But," said the morning Cincinnati paper, with stars in its eyes for Lucas, "Pettit never worked harder for them."

The locker room was surprisingly quiet, though. Lucas sat on a bench before his locker, his uniform still on and the thick chest hairs bristling wet under his jersey. He carefully undid the elastic bandages that were wrapped about both knees. Robertson, his jersey off and uniform shorts unbuckled, sipped a soft drink in front of his locker. McMahon stood with one foot on a bench, reporters around him. He was happy but cautious. The reporters were primarily interested in what would be termed "Lucas's brilliant debut."

"Mechanically," said McMahon, "he's sound. But he still has to work with O on those plays when he moves in and then out of the pivot."

Home to meet Boston the next night.

Last year the Celtics had beaten the Royals 9 times in 12 games during the regular season, but only 4 times in 7 games in the playoffs, which, of course, was sufficient. The Celts were somewhat different from the year before. Bob Cousy, the Celtics' ballhandling star, had retired. K. C. Jones had stepped in to take his place but did not step into his shoes, as far as Celtic coach Red Auerbach was con-

83

cerned. Once at a luncheon, Auerbach listened to a college coach who said he had a player who was "another Cousy." Auerbach, out of turn, stood and said, "I'm getting tired of this baloney. You don't know how many times I hear it. Every kid who can dribble a ball gets called as good as Cousy. Well, I've got news for you. There ain't nobody as good as Cooz."

Cousy was a remarkable player with an ability to throw magical passes before 10,000 people with 20,000 popping eyes. But one player was now gaining on him, had even surpassed him according to some observers. "Oscar," said Dick McGuire in 1961, when he coached the Detroit Pistons, "is better than Cousy ever was. Oscar is the finest player in basketball."

And Cousy himself said, "Robertson is the best of his kind ever to come into the league." But the thought of someone being better stimulated Cousy, just as it has spurred Robertson.

After a game in 1961 in which Cousy played to his peak, amazing opponents and fans alike with his passing and shooting, Cousy admitted that his incentive was printed in that afternoon's newspaper. A sportswriter had stated that, though Cousy was flashier than Robertson, "there seems to be growing sentiment in the league that Robertson is the equal of or better than Bob in almost every other phase of the game. Oscar is a better shooter, better and more useful defensively, better rebounder and his equal as a feeder."

Now Cousy was gone. In a sense his leave-taking would make it harder on Robertson. K. C. Jones would be assigned to guard Robertson and would sometimes be aided by two or even three other players, which was not unusual. Sam Jones had formerly been given the task of guarding Robertson. (Although Auerbach would say that he would ask his starting five which one wanted to guard Robertson. None did.

But the one with the worst excuse got him.) And Sam Jones was good. But K.C. was possibly the finest defensive guard to ever play in the NBA.

"K.C.," said Tom Hawkins, "could harass a rattlesnake. He was tenacious. He stayed in a man's jock."

Robertson always gave K.C. his due, though Oscar's confidence and pride—and sheer skill—would not allow him to admit that anyone could stop him.

"The best you could ever hope to do against Oscar," K.C. had said, "was to hold him below his average. That's all. You couldn't stop him per se. He just had too many moves."

Cousy was never thought of as a formidable defensive player, despite pyrotechnical steals on occasion. So the Celtic defense (which already had three of the best in the league—Russell, Satch Sanders and John Havlicek) was improved. Cousy's departure also gave Bill Russell more incentive, though the insuperable Russell hardly needed it. Ever since he had come to Boston he was always the "second star" on the team, despite the fact that before his arrival Boston had never won a championship. Now, as the 1963-64 season began, he had played seven seasons and the Celtics had been world champions in six of them. (The only time they lost, 1957-58, Russell sprained an ankle and did not play in the last two games of the championship finals against St. Louis. Boston lost both of those games, each by 2 points. No one doubts Russell would have at least made up that minuscule difference. St. Louis won the series, 4 games to 2.)

All six of those championships, though, were won with Cousy in the backcourt. Russell felt that he had something to prove this season, that the Celtics were champions primarily because of Russell in the pivot feeding off unselfishly and scaring the shoelaces off opponents, who hurried their shots when they saw his cobra-quick arms.

85

"Bob," said Russell, "did more to enhance the game than any other single man." But still . . .

The Celtics had, like the Royals, won their season opener decisively, by 14 points at Baltimore. Now they were in Cincinnati to play the team that was rated their stiffest competition. It was to be the first of twelve regular-season games between them.

Ten thousand and thirteen fans crowded into Cincinnati Gardens on Thursday evening, October 17, setting the local attendance record for a home opener. McMahon believed that defense was the key to beating the Celtics. So he started Bockhorn, his best and most aggressive defensive guard outside of Robertson.

It was a frenetic game, with the lead often changing hands. And it was a sticky defensive game, to be sure. Sanders, bony, gawky-looking yet graceful at 6-6, 210 pounds latched onto Lucas like a barnacle. Lucas did not score a basket in the first three periods. And Robertson was having an unspectacular night. Going into the final quarter the Royals were way behind, 82-65. But with Lucas finally shaking Sanders, Robertson hitting and Arnette zooming in and out stealing balls, the Royals got back in the game and with less than a minute to go needed a basket to tie. Robertson came down court thumping, looking for an opening. K. C. Jones, crouching, backpedaling, never losing his balance, hands slapping at the ball, was with him. Havlicek, streaking from the side, broke in, slapped the ball from Robertson and went in for a big basket. The Royals lost by only a point, 93-92. Robertson had 20 points, but hit only 7 baskets in 23 shots. He pulled down 13 rebounds and had 9 assists. Lucas scored 10 points in the final period and finished the game with 13. But the most decisive statistic was this: 30 rebounds for Bill Russell.

The Royals were disappointed but not despairing. They had lost, but they had come back strong. The team showed it did not fear the Celtics. But one problem persisted. Lucas and Robertson were still having difficulty coordinating on the court. One reason was Lucas. Sam Jones said after the game, "Lucas is hesitant out there. But he can go to the basket to board like Baylor."

Another reason was Robertson. "In fairness to Lucas," wrote a Cincinnati reporter the next day, "the ball was seldom worked into him as Robertson tried to crack the Boston defense with little success."

Robertson believes he can score off anybody, and there are those who agree with him—Richie Guerin, for one. Guerin has said, "Robertson can get off a shot—and I mean a good shot, the shot he wants—anytime he wants to."

McMahon has said, "Another thing. It just doesn't occur to Oscar that someone can take the ball from him. In fact, they can't. Oscar is deadly from about 18 feet on in. But when he gets to 18 feet, he wants the foul line, then 10 feet, and he keeps right on moving in until he forces a double-teaming situation and gets off the pass or the shot he can't miss."

But not tonight. Havlicek took the ball away in a crucial situation. It is to Robertson's credit—but also in his disfavor—that he becomes a human piledriver. There are times when he becomes obstinate, when it is foolhardy to try to drive off Russell. Yet it is still difficult to fault. "I attack the defense," said Robertson. "I try to get my big guys in the play. I penetrate as far as I can to start off."

Tonight the Royals simply started too slowly. In the first 29 minutes of the first half, Twyman and Lucas took but five shots between them, which said something for the Boston defense. It said something about the nailing of

Twyman and Lucas to their spots. And it said something about Robertson handling the ball too much. McMahon said, "They can't shoot without the ball."

As soon as the game ended, McMahon told the players that tomorrow, an off day, there would be practice. It was a long practice, two and a half hours. Emphasis was placed on setting up the forwards, primarily Lucas, with shot opportunities. And there was concentration on passing rather than dribbling. The team looked good, but problems had to be straightened out.

The Knicks came to town the following night and the Royals bombed them. Seven Royals scored in double figures. Oscar led with 19 points, Lucas had 15. Arnette started, was nervous and missed three layups, but scored 9 points and was again ubiquitous on defense. Bob Boozer was also having some good times. As first substitute he was determined to show McMahon in particular and everyone in general that he belonged back in the starting five. In the first three games he had scored 10, 12 and 14 points. "Boozer," conceded McMahon, "has turned in three fine performances." Which pleased Boozer, until the next game when he was again on the bench at tipoff time.

There was a new Wilt Chamberlain this year. And the Royals would meet him in their next game. The San Francisco Warriors' 7-foot-1, 275-pound center had been the league's top scorer from the moment he stepped onto the court in the NBA. But if he was long of leg, he was short of temper. Times were when he would feel piercing elbows and scream that he was being manhandled, and it had affected his game. He was cooler now, more ready to accept the slings and arrows of outrageous play, and more than ready to give it back in kind. But the most important change was that Chamberlain now was a team player. He was passing off. In the previous season he had averaged nearly 45 points per game but his team finished fourth in the Western Division and did not make the playoffs. After five years in the league, Chamberlain had broken almost every scoring record. But a team with Wilt Chamberlain had never won an NBA championship. Like Robertson (and West and Baylor, too), Chamberlain shouldered the criticism that he was not a winner.

Coach Alex Hannum apparently had influenced Chamberlain to consider his teammates, that it was neither fun nor prosperous for them to continue feeding a ball-eating dragon. If they could win, that was one thing, but to not even make the playoffs—that was ludicrous.

Another large crowd, this time 6,417, turned up at the Gardens to see the new Wilt and the new Royals. They were not disappointed. Wilt scored a trifling 36 points and the Royals won, 103-97. Robertson was again the Royals' high scorer with 22 points. Other than Wilt, there was another surprising element in the game. It was Bud Olsen. Olsen, tall, lithe and Nordic, had been so disheartened the year before, his rookie season, that he said he "began to feel like a flunky. I was the only one not playing. I wanted to hide." But tonight he came off the bench to play 19 minutes and, with Chamberlain hovering around the backboards, still took 8 rebounds and scored 11 points, hitting on 5 of 8 shots.

Olsen had played so little the year before that McMahon had him show up at rookie camp this fall. "It didn't embarrass me," said Olsen. "McMahon didn't know what I could do. And it worked to my advantage. I played well. And the first impression is usually a lasting one."

It is never enjoyable nor profitable for a pro-basketball player not to be playing. But Olsen had made the most of it. He took great pleasure in watching Robertson perform. "O always amazes me," said Olsen. "He's always got something new, something different. I'd sit on the bench and see some fantastic move and I'd punch the guy sitting next to me, 'You see that? You see that?' It seemed O never failed to come up with the big play for you. I saw Oscar in high school, and I played against him in college. He just keeps getting better."

Olson recalled a night when his University of Louisville team played the University of Cincinnati. Before the game, Louisville coach Peck Hickman gave a rousing pep talk that ended with, "And remember, Robertson puts on his jockey strap the same way you guys do." After the game, Olsen recalls, the Louisville Cardinals dragged into the locker room. They had been beaten by some 25 points and Robertson had scored at will, passed at will, rebounded at will, stolen balls at will. As Louisville undressed quietly, Ron Rubenstein, a guard, turned to Olsen and said wryly, "I don't care what the coach says, Robertson *has* to put his jockey strap on differently."

Two days off at home. Robertson took this leisure period to announce that Mrs. Robertson was expecting their second child in January; they had one daughter, Shana Yvonne, one and a half years old.

The Los Angeles Lakers were next in town. They had "the three fastest guns in the West," Baylor, West and lefty Dick Barnett—all outstanding shooters and none of them shy about it. Rudy LaRusso was a bruising rebounder with some ability to score. But the Lakers' problem always was an effective big man. Jim Krebs was 6-8, 230, but averaged only 8 points a game the year before and was a lackluster rebounder. Leroy Ellis was 6-10 but only 210, and that tells his story—no beef. Gene Wiley had the same physical statistics as Ellis. Neither had averaged more than three baskets a game the year before. But still the Lakers had taken the Celtics to the final seconds of the sixth and final game of the championship playoffs last season before losing, 112-109. They were rated to be back on top in their division. The Lakers were now 2-1 for the brief season. The Royals were 3-1, but all was not as good as it could be. Robertson and Twyman were both shooting below normal accuracy. Robertson was hitting only .368 percent of his shots, Twyman .333.

The year before, Robertson had broken the Royals' one-season field-goal-percentage record with .518, third best in the league. The record had been held by Twyman, .488 in 1960-61. Now both were obviously off form.

"I'd be concerned," said McMahon, "if we were losing. But I feel that both O and Jack have been working on defense."

Boozer continued to play well, and was shooting at a .513 pace, second on the team to Smith's 58 percent. Yet Boozer was slowly being overshadowed by Hawkins, his roommate and friend. Hawkins was impressive both defensively and under the boards, though he was not scoring in consistent double figures as was Boozer.

The Lakers proved how formidable they were. West scored 27 points, Baylor 22, Barnett and LaRusso 21 in a 122-109 victory. It was a disturbing game for the Royals. Most of LaRusso's points came on offensive rebounds, as he slipped past Lucas here and knocked past him there. LaRusso ended up with 16 rebounds. Jim Krebs said afterward, "The next time a national magazine puts Jerry Lucas on the cover, which is almost about once a week, seems like they're going to have to drape Rudy LaRusso over him so people will recognize him."

The game was little better for Robertson, though he was Royals' high scorer with 27 points. Robertson had made 6 of 10 floor attempts in the first half. In the second half there was an unusual occurrence. Robertson, who usually seems to gather steam in the second half, went cold, hitting on just 2 of 12 shots. And in the last quarter, when the Royals appeared to be making a move, Robertson missed shots and committed ballhandling errors.

The first five games of the season had not been the greatest start for what Robertson hoped would be his greatest season. There had been good news before the game, however. Tom Thacker was being released early from the Army for "occupational reasons." "The Cobra," as they called him, showed up at the Gardens looking fit, trim and mustachioed.

"I know this is a good team," he said, "that's what I'm expecting—a winner the first year. I'm used to those championship teams."

Thacker, 6-2, 170, had played forward for the University of Cincinnati and there learned what championships were all about. He played with two NCAA champions and one runner up. He was All-American for the last two years. Though he was not renowned for his shooting touch, he did manage to become the fourth-highest scorer in school history, behind Robertson, Twyman and Paul Hogue. Thacker had a reputation as a clutch player and did the bulk of his scoring on drives and offensive rebounds. Other assets were passing ability and gritty defense.

With the Royals he would have to make the transition to guard, just as Robertson had. Robertson, though, had always been a ballhandler, Thacker less so. It was good to have Thacker. He brought the aura of a winner with him. And the Royals, with three of their top players slumping, needed the lift.

Thacker was with the team as they boarded an early-morning flight for a game the next night in San Francisco. It was a 2,000-mile trip after an exhausting night game. The weary travel of the NBA grind was beginning. This road trip shaped up thusly: two games in San Francisco, with two off-days in-between; the fifth day in Los Angeles for a night game, then a day off; a game the following night, again, against Los Angeles; a flight to Dayton, Ohio, for a game against Philadelphia; then to Boston to play the Celtics. Then, at long last, home again.

The trip started off poorly, with a 102-99 loss to the Warriors. Games against the Warriors were physically debilitating. Chamberlain alone could wear a team down by simply tramping onto the court. Playing against him, particularly the way Embry did, presented an almost comical picture: two mammoth creatures grunting and straining against each other like the classic, motionless, unrelenting death struggle of two walruses.

10

Jack Twyman fractured two bones in his left hand. Odie Smith severely sprained an ankle. Warrior forward Tom Meschery crashed to the floor and it took ten stitches to darn his forehead. It had been a rough game.

The Royals won this, the second game at San Francisco, but there are times when one can be justifiably skeptical about a scoreboard. Twyman was rounding into form before the injury. In the last two games he had hit on 22 of 37 field-goal attempts. The injury was a blow to the team, a personal blow. Twyman was proud of his consecutive-game string and had played with all types of physical misery in the last nine years to maintain it. He had been in 609 straight NBA games, second among active players to the 678 of Johnny Kerr of Philadelphia, and third lifetime to

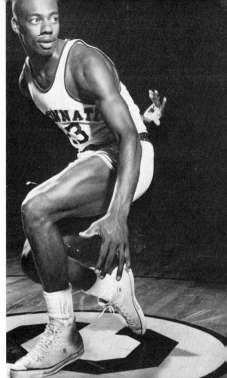

Oscar Robertson, star backcourtman of the Cincinnati Royals.

A young Oscar Roberston, working in the Accounting Department of the Cincinnati Gas and Electric Company, while a co-op student at the University of Cincinnati. (UNITED PRESS TELEPHOTO)

A news picture of Oscar when he was a sophomore basketball sensation at the University of Cincinnati. He had just scored 37 points in a game against the University of Houston to take the national scoring lead from Wilt Chamberlain. (UNITED PRESS TELEPHOTO)

Jerry Lucas pulls down rebound as Oscar looks on. (MALCOLM EMMONS)

Oscar and Roy Campanella with Maurice Stokes prior to an annual Stokes Benefit game. (GEORGE KALINSKY)

New York's Cazzie Russell guards Oscar. (GEORGE KALINSKY)

Oscar gets off a shot against Dave Stallworth of the Knicks at Madison Square Garden. (GEORGE KALINSKY)

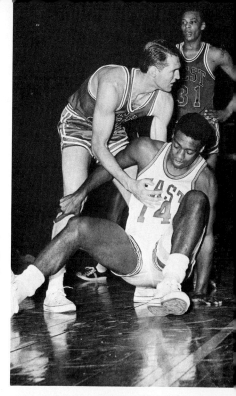

Oscar being helped up by Jerry West after a fall during the 1969 All-Star game. (GEORGE KALINSKY)

Oscar trying to drive past a close-guarding Jerry West in All-Star game. (GEORGE KALINSKY)

Oscar walks off Madison Square Garden court after his last game as a Cincinnati Royal. (GEORGE KALINSKY)

Oscar goes up for a layup against the New York Knicks in 1968.
(MALCOLM EMMONS)

Oscar being presented with trophy for most valuable player by Commissioner Walter Kennedy in 1969 All-Star game. (GEORGE KALINSKY)

the retired Dolph Schayes of Syracuse, who held the record with 706. Twyman's string and hand were broken when Wayne Hightower, scrambling, fell hard on the ball. Twyman's hand was underneath the ball.

Meschery's injury was rather embarrassing. Robertson was going about stealing the ball from him and Meschery frantically dived to retrieve it. He flumped forward with a boom, perforating his skull.

The Royals left San Francisco. Tomorrow night, Los Angeles. The Lakers were a superior shooting team, so the Royals needed points against them. It was disheartening that two of their best shots—Smith and Twyman—would be out. Injuries, though, are as much a part of the NBA as is smog of L.A. A sprained ankle, as Smith suffered, is expected. But a fractured hand is harder to take. To win a championship, or to even be in contention, a team must be lucky as well as extremely skilled. ("It is not always the best team that wins," Robertson has said.) Fortunate breaks (as opposed to a break like Twyman's) are necessary: referee decisions, an opponent injured, a man accidentally in the right place to pick off a full-court pass, a shot that balances on the rim —while ten men watch, agape, like a crowd entranced by a man on the ledge of the fortieth floor—then drops in.

So when a key player incurs an injury, understandably a newspaper reports the following day that Twyman's fracture "is a cruel blow to Cincinnati's lofty expectations." A cast was put on. Doctors said he would be out of action three to six weeks. As it turned out, Twyman missed twelve games, nearly four weeks.

Fourteen thousand five hundred and thirty-three persons with as many leather lungs jammed into the Los Angeles Sports Arena. But for Embry it was like emerging into the clearing from a forest: Wilt Chamberlain was now but a nightmarish memory. For Lucas, though, the Lakers meant LaRusso. And for Robertson it was a personal challenge. While in every game he had to prove he was the best, the Lakers were something special. For among those who did not consider Oscar the best all-around player, some thought that West was and others Baylor.

And it was quite a game. Whenever the Royals appeared set to pull away, Jerry West would hit a jump shot. Tom Thacker got his first taste of NBA frustration when he was used in the second half to guard West. All Thacker got for his efforts was a closer vantage point in which to view the expertness of West. Since Cincinnati stayed ahead, Robertson, in order to concentrate on offense, did not guard West. West was high scorer with 37 points, with Robertson right behind with 36. Thacker scored on a free throw. The Royals won, 115-107.

"But it was Embry," said Laker coach Fred Schaus, "who killed us." Embry got 15 rebounds, and scored 30 points; after Chamberlain, Embry was like a bully in a playground.

The game was also important for Lucas. He outscored and outrebounded LaRusso, scoring 18 points to LaRusso's 8, and grabbing 11 rebounds to LaRusso's 10. Lucas missed just 2 of 10 shots from the floor.

The Royals' *joi de vivre* was stifled by the Lakers two nights later when Embry fouled out, Robertson got into foul trouble and played only 13 minutes in the first half because of it and the Royals lost. Robertson still managed 26 points.

Two nights later, Philadelphia in Dayton. NBA teams often play from a handful to a third of their "home" games on the road in hopes that fans in another city will flock to the local arena to see a regular-season pro game. The Royals scheduled games regularly in Indianapolis (Robertson's home town) and would do the same in following years at Columbus (to take advantage of Lucas' popularity there). Dayton was an ideal stop for the Royals, so two games were scheduled there this year. Dayton is some 40 miles north of Cincinnati, and there was much local interest in the Royals. Bockhorn had played college ball there and Bud Olsen high school ball. Lucas' home was in nearby Middletown and Embry was familiar as a state high school star as well as an opponent with Miami University. These factors did not escape the Royals' schedule-maker.

The Philadelphia 76ers were much the same team that had managed to hold on to second place in the Eastern division despite an inspired late-season rush by the Royals. But there was one major difference. Schayes had retired as player and was now the coach. Stars for Philadelphia were guard Hal Greer, an uncanny outside shooter; center Johnny Kerr, a large redhead with a kindly disposition except when he saw a ball bouncing off a backboard; Chet Walker, a rookie forward last season who was now averaging in double figures; and guard Larry Costello, one of the best defensive backcourtmen in the game.

At Dayton, both teams were cold from the floor. Shots struck the rim with a clang, as though a lid were on it. The Royals shot 32 percent, the 76ers 35. Arnette said afterward, "I've gone zero for 10 before, but in baseball not basketball." Even Robertson had problems and missed 4 of 9 free throws. Embry fouled out for the second successive game. So did Lucas, after grabbing 17 rebounds. With the score 86-83 in the Royals' favor and less than 3 minutes remaining, Robertson hit three straight clutch shots and Bob Boozer scored on two free throws, so with only 29 seconds left the Royals had the game, 94-89. Robertson scored 25 points, and when league statistics were released on the following day, Robertson was high scorer. He had 248 points. He was also No. 1 in assists, with 100. Lucas was the rebound leader.

(But the Royals had an advantage in that they had played ten games while the other clubs had played only six to nine.)

Though the Royals had won 6 of 10, they would pick up the papers and look at the standings and close their eyes. It seemed as if there were three leagues in the NBA. There was the Western Division, with Los Angeles, San Francisco and St. Louis in contention. There was the Eastern Division, with the Royals and Philadelphia as staunch contestants for league honors. Then there was the Boston Celtics, a one-team league. The Celtics had played seven games and won seven games. And only Cincinnati, with a 1-point loss, had even come close to defeating them. Last season the Celtics had lost only 22 regular-season games, and the year before that they had been defeated only twenty times. No one seriously thought they would go through a season undefeated. That was ridiculous. It was impossible. The NBA was too tough, too well-balanced. Somebody had to beat them. But who? When? The Royals had the answer, they hoped.

The Royals flew to Boston for their first game of the season at the Celtics' home. McMahon still felt that the forwards were not seeing the ball enough. "We still have to get the ball ahead to our forwards rather than have Oscar try to dribble it up," he said. So it was hardly a coincidence that in the next game against Boston, Robertson started the game at forward.

"I felt," said McMahon, shuttling the issue a bit, "that our offense was being slowed anyway by teams double- and triple-teaming Oscar. They were bottling him up outside. So I thought that at forward he would be in offensive position as soon as he got the ball."

Hawkins and Bockhorn brought the ball up instead. But this did not work and Boston won easily, 139-121. Without Robertson handling the ball the Royal offense slowed to a walk. Robertson returned to guard. And that's where he was two nights later when the Royals again met the Celtics, this time in Cincinnati Gardens. The game was a scramble from the start. With seconds remaining before the end of the half, Robertson made one of the most sensational shots of his sensational career. He stole the ball and threw up a 50-foot hook shot from the half-court line that dropped through the net as the buzzer sounded.

The Royals, however, fell further behind and the score was 107-93 with 6½ minutes remaining in the game. Then they scored on nine straight free throws. Robertson hit a jump shot from the baseline and Embry scored on a short jump shot after Robertson had driven in and passed off. Now it was 107-106, Celtics. Then Boston scored 5 points in a row: 112-106. Again the Royals battled back. With 21 seconds left, Boozer hit a long corner shot and the Royals led, 114-113. But Sam Jones banked a jump shot from 25-feet out and the Celtics, with seconds left, looked like winners.

The Royals took it out and there was confusion like nothing since Orson Wells told the nation the Martians were coming. Robertson somehow saw Boozer and zipped him a pass, and Boozer came through again—this time from 15-feet out as the crowd nearly blew the roof off. Then Heinsohn's hook shot at the buzzer missed. Yes, finally, the Celtics lost!

There was jubilation in the Royals' locker room. "The sweetest victory we've ever had," said Robertson. And he was smiling broadly, with his cheeks round and boyish and catching the light from the ceiling.

"What about that hook shot, Oscar?" he was asked above the din.

"I didn't aim. I didn't have time . . . just threw it. Someone upstairs had to give me some help on that."

"That's the one that beat them," called Lucas, grinning.

So the Celtics were not unbeatable, and the Royals had nine more times to prove it. Sure, it had taken a super effort by Robertson, who scored 35 points and hit on half of his 26 shots from the field. And it took nervy play by Boozer, who hit the last two crucial shots and scored all of his 10 points in the last quarter. But they could do it. First place was now a realistic goal.

First place was important for three reasons. More money was one: finish first and the team splits $7,500; second place is worth only $3,500. Second, the league champion gets a rest in the first round of the playoffs and the second and third-place teams battle to decide which plays No. 1; then the best-of-seven series for the league title begins in the winner's home and—if it goes seven—the first-place team has the home-court advantage four times, including the first and seventh games. Third, the first-place team has an obvious psychological lift.

Beating the champions was more than a lift for the Royals. It was a ride on a magic carpet of dreams. And Detroit would feel the effects. The Pistons came to town next, and with rather sorry credentials. They had lost 5 of 7 games and were last in the West. Star forward Dave De Busschere was out with a broken leg, forward Bailey Howell, team high scorer the season before, was playing little, seemed discontent and there were rumors of a trade for him. Don Ohl, good-shooting veteran guard, was not going well.

So it was that Charley Wolf came back for the first time since leaving the Royals to coach the Pistons. Detroit, with its veteran players, did not then appear to be taking to Wolf's stringent methods with glee. The team that Wolf was so instrumental in developing over the last three years, and which had come from last place to be a surprise contender under him, now was a talented, maturing, respected team, one of the best in basketball. Meanwhile, Wolf was practically starting all over with a loser. Detroit had finished third in the West the previous year and won only 1 game in 4 against St. Louis in the first-round of the playoffs last year. And with injuries, with grumblings, they were now even weaker—and they looked it as the Royals beat them, 118-109. Robertson scored 28 points, Lucas 22 points (plus 25 rebounds) and Embry 30 points. But then San Francisco came in and beat the Royals, 98-92.

The Royals next game was in Madison Square Garden against the Knicks. The Garden stood alone in American indoor sports. It had a mystique constructed by its history of famous championship boxing fights and legendary basketball games. And it was in New York. With the nation's communications media centered in New York, an event in that town took on greater importance.

"Everything outside of New York," a writer once said, "is Bridgeport." Whether this is true does not matter here. What is significant is that New Yorkers believe it, and they tend to convince a lot of people.

Robertson was leading the nation in scoring when he had first come to New York as a collegian in 1958. He felt the skepticism there about him. Like so many others, Robertson wanted to prove himself in New York, in the Garden, against Seton Hall. Oscar was tense before the game and is supposed to have told someone, "I hope I don't goof up." (Later he admitted that he was not as nervous as before his first varsity game a month earlier, against Indiana State, when, after a jittery 7 minutes, he warmed up and scored 28 points.)

The Seton Hall game was one of the highlights of Robertson's career. He scored 56 points and broke the Garden scoring record as the Bearcats won, 118-54.

"Robertson," said Joe Lapchick, former star of the Original Celtics and then coach of St. John's, "is the best sophomore I've ever seen. He could become the greatest player, too. . . . He showed me every shot in the book—from everywhere. I'd say he had the best scoring touch since Hank Luisetti. I feel he could make the pros right now because he can do everything besides the shooting."

The St. Louis Hawks were in town and some players attended the game. One was Jack McMahon. He was asked if he thought Robertson would make a pro.

"Are you kidding?" replied McMahon.

Reporters got another side of Robertson when they talked to him in the locker room afterward. It was a reticent, monosyllabic Robertson, neither eager nor interested in the kind of superficialities that often pass for questions in postgame interviews. He also may not have known what was expected of him. When asked how he felt about the record, he answered, "I was glad."

A few more such questions and a few more such answers followed. One writer summed up the impression of the young man: "Oscar makes Calvin Coolidge sound like a blabbermouth."

Robertson played in the Garden in each of his three college years. And each year he returned after the season to the annual Basketball Writers' dinner to accept the trophy for "Best Visiting Player."

In New York now, McMahon made note that the Detroit game had been significant for the way Robertson and Lucas worked pick-and-roll plays, especially in the heat of Detroit's pressing defense. McMahon also told reporters how much Boozer has meant to the club: "He's done well for us all year. He has been the key man off the bench and in 28 minutes against Detroit he hit on 6 of 11 from the floor and scored 16 points."

As for the Knicks, they had recently obtained Bill (The Hill) McGill, 6-9, from Baltimore, and Len Chappell, 6-8 from Philadelphia. With these two additions, said McMahon, "they have shed the patsie tag." They did for this game, at any rate. Knicks, 122; Royals, 114.

Health problems were now debilitating the Royals. Arnette had the flu, Twyman was still out with the fractured hand, Smith was still sore from an ankle sprain, as was Hawkins, and Boozer had a bruised left leg. Also, Bockhorn's father-in-law had died and Bockhorn returned home for the funeral. Canes and casts were becoming standard traveling equipment with the Royals.

A strange thing happened in their next game, in Baltimore the following night. For the last 3 minutes and 11 seconds of the game the Royals made only one field goal, and that was on goaltending called against Walt Bellamy on a Robertson shot. The Royals had a 108-99 lead when the cold spell set in, yet Gene Shue had a chance to tie the game in the last seconds. He had two free throws coming with the score 110-108. He made the first but missed the second, and Lucas got the rebound and passed to Robertson, who dribbled out the clock.

The Royals went back to New York to play Detroit in one-half of a doubleheader. Charley Wolf was thrown out of the game for protesting a call and, to add fuel to his fire, the Royals beat the Pistons, 127-102. It was a loosely played game but, before departing, Wolf was able to see enough to say that this was Oscar's best game so far this season. Robertson scored 32 points (hitting on 10 of 16 from the floor) and had the sensational total of 21 assists.

The Royals watched part of the second game before departing for Detroit, where they had a game the following night. It would have been better for their morale had they just dressed and left. The Celtics whipped New York,

126-98, for their twelfth win of the season against just that one Cincinnati loss. The Royals were now in second place with a 10-8 record, 4½ games behind the league leaders. Philadelphia and New York followed in that order, both with losing records. In the West, St. Louis and Los Angeles were tied for top spot with 9-6 records.

11

Oscar bellowed. He stamped his feet like an adagio dancer. He shook his fists furiously. It was his sixth foul and, for the second game in a row, he was disqualified. He did not want to leave the Cobo Arena court. The Royals had fought back from a 105-99 deficit and were 1 point down, 110-109, to the Pistons. There were 4½ minutes left in the game. Piston guard Don Ohl was shooting and Robertson broke through a pick to block the shot. A whistle. A scream. A stamp.

"You were five guys away," shouted Robertson at referee Sid Borgia. "This referee, this one was closer, he didn't call it. What is this? You can't call that! You didn't see it! You weren't near it!"

Another whistle. Technical foul on Robertson. Robertson

howled, snorted and, with much tossing of head and shaking of fist, grudgingly stomped back to the bench.

It was the second time this season that Borgia, recently named head of NBA officials, had worked a Cincinnati game in which he had been so violently tongue-lashed. In San Francisco earlier, Alex Hannum had leaped off the bench at a Borgia call. A technical was called. Shortly after, another foul, another Hannum leap, another technical. Two technicals and the culprit is ejected, according to league rules. In a rage afterward, Hannum spluttered, "Borgia's flipped his lid since becoming head of officials. And who was that other ref? Sam Taub? A rookie! He's probably refereed some junior high school ball."

Refereeing is a thankless job in the NBA. And a virtually impossible one. In Holiday Magazine, writer Jeremy Larner described it this way:

> The no-contact rule is purely theoretical, a platonic ideal that can be approached only by the desire of the players themselves. Decent players have to *want* to avoid unnecessary contact; if they don't no referee can control the game. The best a ref can do is call a significant selection of fouls rather than every one.
>
> "The violence is nearly continuous; an attempt to penalize all of it would bring the game to utter standstill. Thus all too often games are won in the last moment by fluke rather than skill—by a harassed referee seeing countless fouls and deciding by mental coin-flip to call one and ignore the rest.

Oscar, in particular, is probably as harassed, slapped, jabbed as any other single player. He is a threat who can score off anyone and is as dangerous when not shooting as when tossing the ball up. Thousands of minor fouls are committed on him in every game. Conversely, he commits his share of offensive and defensive protective illegalities. When he first came into the league, in fact, he brought with him the wiliness necessary for survival: a finger in the rib of a rival shooter; a sharp right elbow to protect the ball being dribbled with the left hand; holding a man by the seat of his pants under the backboard. Robertson also was adept at putting his hand on a man's hip and swinging himself around his rival for rebounding position.

"Someone," said Dolph Schayes, "is going to grab that arm someday and throw Robertson into the third row."

"You've got to know where the referee is," said Tom Heinsohn.

"It angers me," said Robertson, "that when you're playing tough—pushing, shoving, hands on guys—and they call it on you but not on them. They aren't consistent. I mean, a guy will run through a pick, right through. No call. Then you go down to the other end and do the same thing and they call a foul on you! Sure, it's tough. And there are some good officials, but it's not as good as it should be overall. I know the tempo is much faster in basketball than in baseball or football. But they're getting paid and they should do the job."

"We don't call a foul," said one official, "unless the contact directly involves the play—except once in a while. If we called them all, we'd be blowing those damned whistles all night."

Robertson also admits that he hollers at referees to make sure they know he is around. He feels that the players who do not gripe are the ones who are fouled most and without receiving compensatory free throws. "And if you get fouled and there is no foul called," said Robertson, "then it's no foul, right?"

Don Ohl was as persistently rugged a defender as anyone who was assigned to cover Robertson. Ohl's exorbitant use of hands was usually irksome to Robertson. And this night in Detroit the holding and slapping was rough on both sides. But Oscar was getting called for it. And so were the other Royals. Soon Bockhorn fouled out. And Embry, Lucas and Olsen had five fouls apiece. But when Robertson left the Royals disintegrated and lost, 124-118.

The Royals third straight game against the Pistons was postponed. No one had any stomach for sports. It was Friday night, November 22, 1963. President Kennedy had been assassinated and the Royals' executives locked up Cincinnati Gardens and, like the rest of the nation, went home with their thoughts.

The Royals lost to St. Louis, 133-121, despite 33 points by Robertson. Cincinnati's record was now 10-9, and it had lost two straight games. The Royals returned to Cincinnati with the Hawks for a game the next night and, as it turned out, the start of a five-game winning streak in six days. It also marked Twyman's return.

The Royals beat the Hawks by 9, took a day of rest, then flew to New York for the first game of a doubleheader against San Francisco. The Royals were ahead, 86-83, at the end of the third quarter. Robertson scored 13 points in the last quarter and stole the ball repeatedly, controlling and clinching the game as the Royals won, 123-112. At Baltimore they won by 3 points. On to Philadelphia, where the Royals took their fourth by 15 points and Robertson scored 38 and had 16 assists. Lucas, though, was the talk of Convention Hall. With his remarkable ability to time the ball off the boards, and demonstrating more muscle than at almost any time during the season, Lucas pulled down 31 rebounds to break the club record of 30 set in 1957 by Stokes. Lucas also scored 21 points. It was the club's most successful road trip ever.

In Cincinnati less than 24 hours later, Lucas again broke the record. He had 33 rebounds. He scored 25 points, his best scoring night of the season. It was a good night for Twyman, too, despite playing with a cast. He scored 17 points. Robertson scored 29 points in 31 minutes and then rested much of the last quarter as the Royals easily beat the Knicks, 135-110, for their fifth straight win, one short of the club record.

A day off followed. It was a good time for McMahon to sit back in the Royals' office and prop his feet on a desk. "We have," he said with some understatement, "a lot of momentum and confidence now. The boys believe in themselves."

Robertson had scored 691 points in 26 games and was the league leader, as he was in assists. He had a 27.6 scoring average. Chamberlain, though, had a better game average, 32.2, but had played in seven fewer games. Lucas was the league's top rebounder with a 17.1 average. Yet, amid all this bountiful success, there remained one nagging canker. The Celtics refused to lose. Now, as December rolled in, the Celtics were 15-1, 3½ games ahead of the Royals. The Royals' five-game winning streak had cut a mere half game off Boston's lead. But they couldn't worry about the Celtics, not too much, anyway. Self-preservation is the law of the NBA. If you look off in the distance and drop your guard, you are attacked.

And that's what happened on December 1 in Cincinnati Gardens. The Lakers came to town and snapped the Royals' winning streak, 114-109. Robertson also put an end to a personal streak. He had broken his own club record of 35 straight free throws in the game, but missed after his thirty-eighth. He also scored 30 points, but there was nothing newsworthy about that anymore.

The Royals had three days off, and they used it to prepare for the Celtics, who were coming to town on December

5. In practice sessions they continued to work on getting the ball to the forwards. They also worked on clearing a side to let Robertson work one-on-one against K. C. Jones, or anyone else they might have on him. The Celtics were doing more switching on Robertson. They'd let K.C. handle him. Then put a fresh Havlicek against him. Then Sam Jones would get the assignment. And they would double- and triple-team him whenever there was trouble. The idea was to try to wear Robertson down.

The Celtics were not about to let Oscar go one-on-one if they could help it. Though Embry would try to lure Russell out of the pivot to give Robertson room, Russell would still not stray too far from the basket.

"One-on-one, Oscar is the best I've ever seen," said K. C. Jones. "And that's the idea of the game. To isolate your man and beat him. Then you've got a free shot or you've forced a double-team, opening up a teammate for an easy basket. And Oscar is the deadliest shooter and the top passer in this situation. That's why he's the best."

On a one-on-one, Robertson often turns his back to his man, dribbling hard, faking with shoulders and head, moving relentlessly in, in, in. In high schools and colleges throughout the country, coaches admonish their players not to turn their backs to the basket because they can't see the rest of the floor and an opponent can whiz in and steal the ball.

"Sure," said Oscar, "I get the ball stolen sometimes. But I keep my head up. I see my man, and I'm consciously watching his reactions on my moves, waiting for him to commit himself, but I'm also watching the rest of the players out of the corner of my eye. It's been effective for me. The thing is, you just can't be afraid to fail. If the ball is taken away once, it doesn't mean it'll happen again. You have to be aggressive and confident."

His persistence was once noted by Dick Barnett. "If you give Oscar a 12-foot shot, he'll work on you until he's got a 10-foot shot. Give him 10, he wants 8. Give him 8, he wants 6. Give him 6, he wants 4. Give him 4, he wants 2. Give him 2, you know what he wants? That's right, baby. A layup."

There is a story about how Oscar's competitive zeal rises when the ball is stolen from him. A bustling NBA rookie supposedly committed this act. Robertson got so incensed that he came down and scored three straight 3-point one-on-one scores off him. The rookie's coach had two standing rules after that. First, never get Robertson angry. Second, when he is angry, the three closest teammates must forget everything else they are doing and come over to help the poor fellow who is guarding him.

"Always," said Robertson, "play like you mean it."

The Royals were now employing a 3-2 offense, as opposed to the standard two forwards, one center, two guards. Lucas was sent into the pivot to create a double post with Embry. The other forward would go out front. It was McMahon's theory that a low double post would get Lucas into the game more by having his back to basket, the position he was most familiar with. This strategy also left more room in the middle for Oscar—though it was used sparingly against Russell and the Celtics.

The Celtics, in their four games before coming to Cincinnati, had held New York, Los Angeles, Philadelphia and San Francisco, to less than 100 points each and had won by 28, 38, 24 and 13 points, respectively. Only one team had come closer than 6 points to them all season—Cincinnati, and twice. It was a superlative start, a superlative record, and elicited discussion that the Celtics were a better team without the flamboyance of Bob Cousy. Was Cousy overrated? Probably not, though it is certain that the Celtics were a better defensive team without him. Havlicek, a rookie who had averaged 14 points a game last season, was developing into the team's high scorer and was a demon on defense with an almost tireless pursuit. He took up a slack. As did the defensive wizardry of K. C. Jones. And Willie Naulls was shooting the net to shreds. And as always, of course, there was the looming presence of Bill Russell.

But the Royals were hot, too. They were in a groove, and they were home. The home court is usually of great importance in basketball. The partisan crowd surely makes a difference. So does the familiarity of the court. You get to know the spots on your backboard. Maybe your rim is screwed on tighter, or looser, and you get the feel of it. Yet for all these aspects the home-court advantage remains mystical, magical, but nonetheless factual.

And it worked for the Royals, but it got some help from Robertson. The Royals won, 118-108. Oscar played 48 minutes, scored 48 points (one less than his personal high set in November 1961 against Philadelphia), grabbed 11 rebounds and had 7 assists.

"That was the greatest game I've ever seen Robertson play," said Auerbach afterward.

Robertson was asked if in fact it was the best he had ever played. He sat on a steel folding chair before his locker and untied his shoes and looked up with those large eyes, tired now but happy, and said, "I'm not sure if it's one of my best games."

He was serious. He knew it was not a perfect game for him. He remembered that a pass did not hit a man as precisely as he had intended. Sure he had hit on 12 of 12 free throws, but he had missed eleven shots from the field (that he had made eighteen was another matter), and some of those he felt he should not have missed. Maybe he could have dribbled closer to the hoop.

Both teams packed their bags and caught a late plane for

Boston, where they would play the following night. Bone-weary after a hard day's night, they flew off, sinking into the cushy seats of the quietly lighted plane in the floating blackness of night. At such times, Robertson would lean back and maybe be sitting next to one of the black players —Embry or Boozer or Hawkins—and reminisce above the low moan of the motor about his days growing up in Indianapolis and playing basketball in the "Dust Bowl" with his brothers Bailey and Henry, and playing baseball and touch football, which would turn into tackle and wind up with some blood spilled on the asphalt street.

Oscar Palmer Robertson was born November 24, 1938, on his grandfather's sparse farm near Charlotte, Tennessee, the youngest of three boys. When he was three the family moved to the west side of Indianapolis. The neighborhood was a typical big-city ghetto, with ramshackle shingle houses and a dearth of greenery. The Robertson home had four rooms and a tar-paper roof. A coal pit was nearby. Oscar's father worked for the city sanitation department.

Robertson got his first taste of chucking a ball at a basket when he was six after his brother Bailey had nailed up a peach basket behind the house.

"We played with a rag ball held together by elastic," recalls Bailey, "except when we'd get real lucky and find an old broken tennis ball in some alley." When he had no ball to shoot, Oscar would toss tin cans at the basket. At age eight he obtained a small ball that he would meticulously scrub with soap and water every night. His first full-sized ball came when he was eleven. It was brought home by Mrs. Robertson after it had been discarded by the white family for whom she cooked part-time.

The Robertson home was two blocks away from the "Dust Bowl," a little vacant lot where a basketball court had been made. Kids from the neighborhood, including the best players—like Oscar's brother Bailey, who would become a high-scoring star at Indiana State and later play with the Globetrotters, and Willie Gardner, another future Globetrotter, among others—would congregate there. Oscar tagged along with his brothers, but the older boys would not let the little kid into the games.

"Oscar," said Bob Boozer, "liked to tell me how they used to chase him off the court and how he would take his ball and go play by himself."

"I promised myself that I'd get so good they would have to let me play," said Robertson. "I practiced all the time. But I played all other sports, too. Actually, I played more baseball and football than basketball. Well, we didn't have any money and sports was the only outlet I had."

He continued playing basketball a great deal, for basketball is truly the sport of the ghetto. Cars cut down on continuous play of football in the streets, and there is rarely enough grass to go around for sufficient baseball diamonds. Precious little equipment is needed for basketball: hang a basket against a garage in an alley or nail it to a pole in a vacant lot. Get a basketball, any kind—ripped at the seams, scuffed—it doesn't matter. Add a pair of sneakers—everyone has sneakers. You may not have leather shoes for school but you surely have a pair of sneakers. Black kids, especially, have taken to basketball. Maybe, as some scientists have observed, it is because they are better equipped physically than whites to run and jump. Others, though, believe that their success in the game is due to the longer hours they spend at it because of their hunger to do well; all colleges—even Southern ones—are now recruiting basketball players, and these kids know that a basketball scholarship is one of the few sure ways for them to get a college education. (Whatever the reasons, it is a fact that over 60 percent of the NBA players are black, despite the fact that it was not until 1951 that the color bar was dropped in professional organized basketball.)

Robertson played his first organized ball at the Police Athletic League before he was in the seventh grade. And the thin growing boy soon became a standout player. In the eighth grade, in the city public school championship, Oscar led his team to victory. Ray Crowe, who would be Robertson's coach at Crispus Attucks High School, saw the game. It was the first time he had seen Robertson play. "The thing you noticed first about him was his shooting," Crowe remembered. "They'd work the ball around for a last shot in each quarter, give it to him and he'd hit."

As a high school freshman Robertson was 5-8, 160 pounds. He grew 4 inches and gained 15 pounds by his sophomore year. Robertson did not start the first game of his sophomore season, it was the only game in three years of high school varsity basketball he did not start. "It wasn't that he wasn't good enough," said Crowe. "It was simply that we had some seniors. He never played a bad game."

He averaged 12 points a game that first season, then 21.7 the next and 26 as a senior. During summers, Crowe gave Oscar the key to the gym so he could play whenever he felt like it, which was often. Friends have said that when they would drop off their dates at night they would find Robertson alone in the gym working on his dribbling and shooting.

He would not let up, even at home. The thump of a basketball was often heard in the house. "I've got to control it," he would tell Bailey. "I've got to control the dribble."

"You couldn't sleep at night," said his mother, "with that basketball going all the time. Bump! Bump! Bump!"

As is often the case with success stories like Oscar's,

legends develop. One was that he would actually sleep with a basketball. "That's ridiculous," said Oscar. "I mean, does a golfer sleep with his sticks?"

Robertson said he does not recall much about his sophomore season, except that he would practice shooting off the dribble and shooting quickly over defenders. His junior year comes more readily into the focus of recall. It was then that he was the star of the first black team in America to win an open state high school tournament.

The championship game was held at Butler Fieldhouse in Indianapolis. Nine thousand people were there to watch Crispus Attucks against Shortridge. One of the spectators was George Smith, University of Cincinnati coach.

"I took a seat in the stands to watch both teams, but particularly Bill Meriweather, the Attucks' pivot man," Smith later told Jimmy Breslin, then a sportswriter for Newspaper Enterprise Association. "But the first time Robertson put his hands on the ball I forgot everything else. I remember it so well I can diagram it for you even now." (Smith, at a restaurant table, began scribbling on a paper napkin.)

"Robertson came down, then across here from the side on a pick. He made a fake which lifted me out of the seat. Then he gave Meriweather, here in the pivot, a simple hand-off pass for a basket.

"Then Robertson brings the ball down a little later. They pick him up right away. He is dribbling with his right hand. So Oscar changes hands, behind-the-back stuff, and in one motion flips a left-handed bounce pass, perfect lead to it, and some kid scores easily.

"After the game a kid on his team told me, 'With Oscar, you keep your hands up for a pass, even when he isn't looking at you, or you get a flat face.'"

Attucks, however, fell behind 22-9, at the end of the first quarter. Robertson helped bring the team back and it was trailing, 55-54, with little more than a minute left. Robertson waved his teammates to one side, drove and scored. But the Shortridge center, Frank Mead, hit a free throw to send the game into overtime. Soon afterward, Mead hit a field goal with 27 seconds left and Shortridge led, 58-56. Again Robertson worked his way under the basket and scored, tying the score again, and the game went into a sudden-death overtime. Robertson, at 6-3, jumped center against Mead, who was 6-6. Robertson got the tip and quickly the ball was passed to him. He feinted, dribbled in spurts through the tight defense, then stopped at the right of the foul circle, jumped and scored. Attucks, one of only three all-Negro high schools out of 729 schools in Indiana, won the first undefeated state title in the forty-five years of Indiana basketball.

"Oscar was good enough then," said Crowe, "to play pro ball. There were no problems with Oscar. If there was anything I did for him, I think it was to get him to play with others and to think of them, to convince him it was better to be unselfish. When he was a senior and they were double- and triple-teaming him, I told him we could beat anyone we played even if he didn't get a point, if he would just pass off to the open man. He just looked at me and grinned."

Robertson credits Crowe with teaching him more about basketball than anyone else. "And I can never remember him raising his voice," said Oscar. "It didn't impress me much then. I was sort of unimpressionable. Just a kid. But I look back on it now and I can see where it was successful. After all, we only lost one game in my last two years."

Robertson, said Bob Boozer, would also like to reminisce about the two Indiana and Kentucky high school All-Star games played in June of 1956. These are the best high school players from two of the nation's most basketball-mad states

125

KVCC ARCADIA COMMONS
CAMPUS LIBRARY

competing against each other. Robertson dominated both games.

In the first, played in Butler Fieldhouse in Indianapolis before 14,000 fans, Robertson set an All-Star scoring record with 34 points as he led Indiana to a win. But the highlight of the series was to come two days later in the second and final game. Playing in Louisville, the Indiana team was well ahead of Kentucky, 98-70, in the closing minutes. Indiana coach Angus Nicoson had taken Robertson out after he'd scored 37 points. Fans from Indiana were hollering for "100." And the Indiana team had gone cold and seemed unable to score. Nicoson called Robertson over and asked if he could get the 100.

"If I can get my hands on the ball," said Robertson with characteristic honesty and aplomb.

Thirteen seconds remained when Robertson entered the game again. Quickly, he did get his hands on the ball and tossed in a jump shot. He added another field goal as the gun sounded, ending the game. He had scored 41 points, broken the single-game series record for the second night in a row and was unanimously named "Star of Stars."

It came as no surprise to anyone that Robertson, now the most publicized high school player in the nation, would be the target of college basketball recruiters who felt that Oscar could get the best education at their particular school. And, in between classes and studying and geological field trips, maybe even get in some basketball.

A scout from Duquesne was at the game in which Oscar scored his high school high, 62 points. "And he passed off, too!" explained the scout. Afterward, Robertson, according to the scout, asked if he had done anything wrong. Rubbing his hand along his mouth, the scout mumbled something about a minor inadequacy on defense.

"Since I was trying to sign him up," said the scout, "I couldn't very well say, 'You're the most magnificent player I've ever seen. You could go into the pros right now.'"

Besides being a marvelous athlete, Robertson was also a fine student at Attucks. He ranked sixteenth in a class of 171 and was a member of the National Honor Society. Over seventy-five colleges were after him. Indiana University would probably have been Robertson's first choice, but, according to one magazine writer, Robertson harbored a grudge against the school. Two years before, IU had turned down his brother Bailey. At that time, Bailey was believed to be the second-finest high school guard in the state. The best was supposed to be Hallie Bryant, Bailey's teammate. Bailey went on to Indiana Central College and eventually broke the career scoring record for Indiana colleges. Oscar apparently believed that Indiana had turned down his brother because it did not want to bring in two Negro basketball players at the same time. (Indiana, however, in 1953—the year before Bailey Robertson/Hallie Bryant— had recruited and enrolled Charlie Brown and Paxton Lumpkin, two black stars of the sensational all-black Du Sable High School team from Chicago.)

Oscar says he picked Cincinnati because 1) it had a co-op curriculum in which the student alternates between classes and a paying, on-the-job training program over a five-year period, 2) it was relatively close to home and 3) it played a big-time basketball schedule.

During his freshman year, Robertson, who had a 1954 Buick when he entered college, would drive the 110 miles home whenever he could. He missed his friends, his brothers, the city, the high school and, of course, his mother. Mrs. Mazell Robertson has been an important influence on Oscar and his brothers. She is a religious woman who sang with the Beck Jubilee Gospel Singers in Indianapolis, wrote original religious music and has made several television appearances as a singer of spirituals.

"I've always told my boys three things. I want them to believe in God. I want them to be gentlemen. And I want them to be honest," she said.

"I told them the parable about the talents. God gave three men a talent. The first one threw it away and the birds ate it. The second man put his in the sun and it melted. The third man took care of his. The Lord will give you more if you take care of what he gave you."

When the family moved to Indianapolis, Mrs. Robertson was concerned about the unsavory environment of the neighborhood. "There were crap games going on all the time," she recalled. "People were doing all kinds of wrong things, and I had to tell my children why they had to be different, that they could only lose if they did things like that." She also told her children that they had to dream before they could realize their dreams.

When Oscar was eleven his mother and father were divorced. Alone now with her three children, Mrs. Robertson took jobs as a beautician and a domestic. After Oscar made the team at Crispus Attucks, she forced him to quit his paper route. "It wasn't that we didn't need the money," she said, "but he had to get up so early in the morning, and—well, basketball had become so important to him, you see, and it was important that he keep up with his studies, too. You got to give a boy a chance to find himself."

Mrs. Robertson looked after Oscar even when he went to Cincinnati, and she felt that he was not always being understood by the people in whose hands she entrusted him. "There's a lot going on inside Oscar that I don't know," she said, "and there's a lot I do know, but only because I'm his mother and not because he tells me. His coach [George

Smith] doesn't know him and hasn't tried to know him. They know his shots. They know his moves, but they don't know what he's thinking. Sometimes the people in the college act like they own my boy. They don't. I didn't sell him."

Mrs. Robertson had seen few of Oscar's high school games because she had to work, but she did come down to Cincinnati to see some of his college games. She kept apace of his progress. The night he scored 56 points to break the Madison Square Garden record, a reporter called to ask her response.

"Oscar has great respect for the Lord," she said. "I taught him that he can't make it without Him. His faith has carried him as far as he has gone."

Once during Robertson's days at the University of Cincinnati, his mother took ill but had to work, anyway. Oscar told her, "Someday I'll get all those bills paid and sit you down and make you stay there and not work anymore."

Robertson still returns for visits whenever he can. And he enjoys taking some of the black Royals to her home for dinner. She now lives in a modest wood-frame house in Indianapolis.

"Oscar loves to eat," said Bob Boozer, "and he especially likes good soul food. His mother can really cook it, yes indeed. I love going to her house. My favorite is a chess pie. It's sort of a custard. High-caloried but great."

12

While the rest of the workaday world is in midday, professional basketball players are just opening their eyes to the sun that seeps into their hotel rooms. About two-thirty in the afternoon, after the game against Boston in Cincinnati the night before, and the plane ride into Boston following, Robertson and roommate Wayne Embry roused from under their covers. Their uniforms were hanging on chairs to air, and their basketball shoes were open with laces loosened and tongues pulled up to dry out. Nearby, their duffel bags were unzipped.

The two players went downstairs, bought newspapers and had a light brunch. A little later they would eat a full meal, not too heavy, and then not eat again until after the game. They returned to their room and sat around, read the papers, watched television and twirled a basketball around to get the feel back in their fingers. At about 5:30 P.M. they caught a cab for Boston Gardens.

Another packed house, for this was now the most interesting rivalry in the NBA. The Royals were the only team to have beaten the Celtics, and they had done it twice in four games.

The Royals fell 13 points behind at one point in the second half but came back to tie it at 100-100. Then Heinsohn scored 9 straight points to push the Celtics to a 112-107 victory. Robertson had 40 points. The Royals dropped to 3½ games behind Boston.

The Royals packed their bags and, for the second night in a row, grabbed a late plane for a game against New York the next day. They won, 116-105, with Robertson scoring 35 points, getting 15 rebounds and passing off for 14 baskets. Then the Royals hurried to catch another late-night plane and wearily trooped into Philadelphia for their fourth game in four nights in four different cities.

The Royals, obviously showing signs of fatigue, lost to the rugged 76ers, 126-116. Johnny Kerr starred for Philadelphia and scored 33 points, including the 10,000th point of his career. Oscar had 32 points. In the game, Odie Smith and Hal Greer collided head-on and Smith suffered a broken bone under his left eye.

Two days of rest followed—and the Royals needed them. On December 11 they played at Detroit and beat Charley Wolf's Pistons decisively, 127-107. Robertson scored 26 points, but, as it turned out, paid for them. The Royals came home to play New York. This game was notable in that both Robertson and Lucas did not suit up. It was the only game that either would miss during the regular season. Robertson had pulled a muscle in his left leg against the Pistons, and Lucas had aggravated a back condition. The Royals won, anyway, as Twyman led all scorers with 31 points and Embry followed with 26.

Two nights later the Royals returned to Boston and beat the Celtics, 108-105. Oscar and Embry were top scorers with 25 each, and Oscar had a sensational night off the boards, collecting 19 rebounds. But the hero was rookie Tom Thacker, who scored 11 points, all in the last period. The Royals now had beaten the Celtics three times, and those were Boston's only three losses in 23 games thus far. The Royals, meanwhile, had a 20-12 record.

The Royals came home after the game for (incredibly) five days of rest and practice. No games. But something happened the following day that would make a big impact on the Royals. It was Sunday morning, December 15. Bob Boozer woke to the ring of his telephone. The caller was Pepper Wilson.

"Bob," said Wilson quietly, "we've traded you to the Knicks."

Boozer was shocked. He liked Cincinnati and had planned to make it his home; he had also met his future wife, Ella, who lived there. Ballplayers in professional sports are often uprooted in this way, and in most cases it is upsetting. In a sense it involves starting all over again: with a new team, finding a new niche on that team, locating a place to live.

Boozer had not been happy since losing his starting job to Lucas even before the rookie had put on a Royal uniform.

"McMahon didn't have to cater to Lucas and *give* him a spot," said Boozer. "Talent like that is going to win his spot. I got a royal shaft." The pun was intentional and wry.

Boozer also saw an element of race prejudice in the occurrence. "It just seemed to me," said Boozer, "that black players always got screwed there, except for Oscar, of course."

A reporter covering the Royals had noted that McMahon

132

went for beers with some of the white players but "never with the blacks. They would feel uncomfortable in some of the bars that McMahon and the white players stopped off at."

It was neither McMahon nor Wilson who had wanted to make the trade. Tom Grace, years later, took full responsibility for it.

"Boozer was a malcontent," said Grace. "He was a good ballplayer but I just thought he was hurting the club with his attitude. Also, I felt he could profit himself by going to another club. The Knicks were weak and I was sure Boozer could help them."

This was an unusual bit of philanthropy for professional sports, to be sure, but then the unusual was not unique with the Royals' administration. Wilson, however, later said, "The Knicks dangled some money and we bit."

Upon Boozer's departure, McMahon said, "Bob's cooperation was excellent."

Strange statement in light of Grace's remarks. Well, if Grace was determined to get rid of Boozer, then McMahon said he wanted a big man in return. Grace originally wanted Donnis Butcher, a 6-3 forward with New York. McMahon said he was too small. Then Grace arranged a three-way deal which made McMahon, but not Wilson, happier. Boozer was sent to New York, the Knicks then peddled Butcher and 6-3 forward Bob Duffy for guard Johnny Egan and forward Larry Staverman. Staverman was then sent to Cincinnati, along with $15,000, for Boozer.

Staverman, a bright, likable 6-7 forward, was a favorite of Grace. He was a local boy who had played for Charley Wolf at nearby Villa Madonna College. He had started his pro career in Cincinnati in 1958 and played three lackluster years, averaging a little over 4 points a game. He was a rather awkward-looking athlete and did not endear himself to the

Cincinnati fans. He was traded to Chicago in 1962. The following year he moved with them to Baltimore, was traded to Detroit and then returned to Cincinnati to play for his third team in one season.

The Cincinnati fans gave Staverman a rough time, booing him when he came into the game and again whenever he committed an error on the court. Wilson knew their feelings and was against bringing him back. And it seemed that Boozer gained in popularity as soon as 1) he was traded and 2) Staverman returned. Public reaction was unfavorable toward the trade.

Robertson was shocked by the trade. For one thing, he was losing a friend. Their friendship had grown after a rocky start. Oscar had criticized Boozer on the court, as he did most of the other players. "It bites," Boozer had said, "when Oscar makes you look small before 6,000 or 7,000 people. And at one time or another I think he embarrassed every player on the team. He would holler at me and I would holler back. 'Not everyone can be as good as you, Oscar,' I'd say. I mean, the Lord made only one Oscar. But after a while I began to appreciate his tremendous drive to win and I came to know that he meant nothing personal."

Robertson also lost a member of his "own personal ghetto," as Steve Hoffman, then publicity director for the Royals, termed it. According to Hoffman, the black players on the Royals were a close-knit unit, joking together and sharing a mutual understanding that was limited by the boundaries of skin color. Boozer was part of that group. "Oscar was sort of the king, or mogul, of that ghetto," said Hoffman. "He enjoyed kidding the black players especially, and they'd usually go along with it. Sometimes, though, Boozer would get mad and pout—after Oscar would tell him, say, that his method of operating with women was behind the times. But in a day or two it was forgotten."

Robertson would sometimes get the white players into the act. And he might say to one of them, "Let's go out and have some soul food—some good chitlins and greens." The white players might be a bit bewildered by this kind of ethnic reference, but the blacks as well as the whites usually enjoyed the humor. But Robertson took a personal interest in the black players, as would a benevolent ruler in his subjects.

Robertson, said Hoffman, might see a good black player and compare him with some of the white players on the bench and say, "He could help us right now. But when camp opened, a player—black or white—would have to prove himself to Robertson." Robertson had been sold on Thacker, for example. He was a UC man like Oscar, but he was also a winner—having played on two national-championship teams. "He had a lot of backing from O," said Hoffman. And, later on, Thacker had great support from the fans. They would chant, "We want Thacker."

"Unfortunately," said McMahon, "Tom never was an NBA shooter." Oscar would also kid Thacker about his shooting.

(A notable example of Robertson befriending a black teammate occurred several years later with Bob Love. Love was a big, lanky, friendly fellow but rather withdrawn because of a bad stutter. Robertson would bring him out of his shyness by kidding him about many things, including the stutter. It was done in barracks-style humor, coarse and warm. The inference was that the stutter was apparent, so no need to hide it, and it had nothing to do with the kind of man Love was. Love's response was laughter, with a puppy-dog look of respect in his eyes.)

Robertson was upset over the Boozer trade. He felt that Boozer was an important part of the Royals' championship ambitions. "I just couldn't understand that trade," said Robertson years after. Robertson, like Boozer, felt Lucas should have won the job from Boozer on the court. "Bob had started since 1960. I don't know how they could have let him go."

Robertson does have notions, however. He believed there was a quota system in the NBA. "It's hard to determine or seek out," he said, "but I'm sure the guys running the clubs know. We all know it. A lot of good Negro ballplayers should be in the league but generally only four or five spots are open on a team. Boston has five, I think. St. Louis has five. We had five until Boozer was traded. I don't know. It makes you wonder."

Jake Brown, Robertson's lawyer, recalled the time Oscar said to him that there was a quota system in the NBA. "But how can there be?" asked Brown. "Just look at all the black players on the court."

"But look at the bench," said Robertson. "They're all white. You can't tell me that some black players who don't have jobs aren't better than some of those guys sitting on the bench."

Like all professional sports (and that would include the quasi-professionalism of college sports), basketball was slow to admit blacks into its leagues. The first black player signed by an NBA team was Chuck Cooper in 1951. Why were there no black players in professional basketball—other than with the Globetrotters? A trenchant explanation is given by Leonard Koppett in his book, *24 Seconds to Shoot: An Informal History of the National Basketball Association:*

> The [owners] were no more, and no less, enlightened on [the race] question than other promoters of the time: they shared the same context of prejudice that pervaded American society, but as promoters they thought even more specifically and less idealistically. Whatever unconscious motivations may have been at work, on the surface they simply feared change. Would their predominantly white audiences "accept"

Negro stars, and "identify" with them? Today these seem to be naive, simplistic and insincere questions, but they generated real doubts at the time. Whatever else the sports promoters were, they were not social-engineering heroes, eager to take what they saw as a risk in their already shaky enterprise. In this, as in most things, they acted upon expediency as they understood it.

Oscar, like other black kids in a ghetto, was aware of prejudice at a very early age. He knew, as did others in his neighborhood, that there were places in Indianapolis where someone with black skin could not go. There were looks and sometimes spoken asides that told boys like Oscar that they were in alien territory. But Robertson could return to his neighborhood, with all its unpleasantness of poverty but with all the security of familiarity. When he left it for college, he missed it.

In Cincinnati, Robertson for the first time lived in an uncomfortable environment of which he was very wary. He and Roland Shadd, a football player from Pittsburgh, were the first two Negro scholarship students to live in the dorms at the University of Cincinnati. Once, when they were freshmen, they went to a movie theater near the UC campus. "When I got to the window to buy the tickets," said Shadd, "the man said the theater was closed. As soon as I stepped out of the line, he sold a ticket to the next person. I didn't have to be a mindreader to figure that out."

Robertson's two most humiliating experiences in college happened on basketball trips. In his sophomore year the Bearcats flew to Houston for a game there. The team went downtown to the uppercrust Shamrock Hotel. As the red-blazered team checked in, a clerk approached Robertson and said, "You can't stay here."

137

The team stayed at the Shamrock, except for one player—its star. Oscar had to get separate accommodations.

"I didn't know it was going to happen," said Oscar later. "I had no idea. All of a sudden, there it was. I guess the school didn't know, either. They should have known, but I guess they didn't." Later he told a friend back in Cincinnati, "If it happens again I'll be on the bus back to Indianapolis."

The next winter the team again traveled to Houston. This time it stayed together on the university campus.

A year later Cincinnati played in the Dixie Classic, a Christmas holiday tournament in Raleigh, North Carolina. The all-white teams lodged in a plush Raleigh hotel. The teams with black players were put up in North Carolina State fraternity houses. Disagreeable omens were present. Each night as Robertson came onto North Carolina State's William Neal Reynolds Coliseum, packed houses greeted him with taunts.

"It was terrible," recalled Ralph Davis, a white teammate from Kentucky. "They called him all kinds of names. Porter. Redcap. Things like that. It made me sick. I walked over to Oscar and talked with him and tried to help him forget it. The crowd was terrible."

The games were rough, too, and once, Robertson and Dave Budd of Wake Forest tangled and rolled on the floor. Fists flew. No one was hurt, on the outside. Robertson felt that Cincinnati, to prevent such ugly occurrences, should not have scheduled games in such hostile environments. Returning home to Cincinnati after such incidents was not terribly warming for Robertson. Because he was black, he had virtually no campus social life. And he was a loner because of his nature. Throughout his four years at Cincinnati, there were persistent rumors that Robertson had left or was then in the process of stuffing his duffel bag to return to Indianapolis. Coach George Smith was kept in a state of anxiety, and there were times when he would ring up Robertson's room, not get an answer, then practically send out search-and-seizure parties to find out where his star was.

But most of the time Robertson was in his dormitory room. He was majoring in business administration. His grades averaged only C, in comparison with his much better grades in high school. But the motivation was not great for school-work. There was a portable television set in his room, and that gave an indication of Robertson's study habits. Robertson would also dribble a basketball in his room, and Davis, who lived down the hall, said that he knew, when the bouncing had ceased, that Oscar had gone to bed.

Why didn't Oscar go out more? "There's not much of a life for us on campus," said Shadd at the time. "Neither Oscar nor I have ever attended a campus social function. I don't think we ever will."

Oscar agreed. "Why should I?" he asked. "If I go with a date, people are just going to stare at us. And I'm sure not going to find a stag Negro girl at a campus dance."

In professional basketball, Robertson was not confronted with the kind of blatant race experiences he had in college. But the awareness of the problem and the anger about it remains. Robertson has never been able to understand why he or any other man should be looked upon or treated differently because of the color of his skin.

There have been times when Oscar did feel a racial slight face-to-face. For example, when a youth, about thirteen years old, berated Oscar outside a locker room in San Francisco. Robertson had come off the court and did not oblige the youngster with an autograph. Robertson said he would sign after he showered and dressed. The boy began pointing and making derogatory comments.

"He respected me as a ballplayer, but not as a man," said Oscar. "It's true that he was just a kid, but where did he learn such an attitude? From his parents, of course."

Robertson's ire has been stoked by the case of endorsements for black athletes. Few black athletes get the number of endorsements that whites do. This piques all of them. Money is certainly one factor. But another is that the color issue must be brought so close to the playing area. When Robertson first came into professional sports, black athletes received a pittance of endorsements. Things had gotten better by the end of the Sixties, but there were still occasions when Robertson would be turned down for a slacks commercial, for example, because the advertiser was afraid that a black man would hurt the Southern market. In 1964, Robertson, acknowledged as probably the greatest all-around basketball player who ever lived, had one endorsement: a basketball.

He also refused to attend banquets or supermarket openings and the like if he did not receive the kind of remuneration he 1) felt he deserved and 2) found that a white athlete was receiving or had received more money for the same occasion.

Oscar, at times, retains a sense of humor about race. Once, for example, some befogged fan asked him what team he played for. "The Chicago Black Hawks, of course," he said with courtliness.

13

After a sweet six-day layoff, the Royals returned to work and beat the Bullets at the Gardens, 103-96, for their fourth straight win.

The town was excited about their fine team, and now, after fifteen home games, the Royals had drawn 97,419 fans. The year before, despite a rousing finish, the team had drawn 137,739 for 33 games. At their current rate the team would top its 1962-63 attendance figure in six more home games.

The Royals traveled to Baltimore for a game the following night. And their winning streak was snapped. Robertson was held to 8 points during the first three periods, then scored 12 in the final quarter. But Gus Johnson blocked a Royal shot in the last minute and Twyman missed a layup, so the Royals lost, 108-106.

This game was a dramatic example of Robertson's ability to score late in the game, in the clutch. He has a deserved reputation for spurting in the second half. Red Auerbach has a theory about it. "Robertson seems to want to get everybody in the game early," said Auerbach. "He looks to hit every player with a scoring pass in the first half. Then in the second half his game becomes more well-rounded, which means he takes charge. And he begins to look for openings for himself. The other players also count on him in the crucial stages. And why not? Who else would you rather have to lead your attack in the tough stages?"

On that same night, Saturday, December 21, something unusual happened in New York. The Celtics lost their first game against someone other than the Royals. The Knicks beat them, 127-117. A note of interest to the Royals and their fans was that Bob Boozer had scored 19 points and pulled down 22 rebounds. The Celtics were now 23 and 4. It gave the Royals hope, however short-lived, that someone else could beat the Celtics. But on the night the Celtics lost, so did the Royals. And they were unable to pick up ground in the standings.

Home again four nights later, the Royals began another four-game winning streak. They beat St. Louis as Robertson scored 37 points and had 16 assists. Two nights later Boston came to Cincinnati. There were 14,141 people in the stands. The Royals won, 91-87, in a typically tough defensive game. Robertson scored 37 points, had 11 assists and the incredible number of 22 rebounds. And yes, Bill Russell was in the game. Afterward, Jack Twyman said, "Oscar is the only player in the league who can completely control a game. At any given time, he can make a basket, set up a basket or, if needed, grab a rebound. There weren't any easy shots tonight. You had to shoot 'em through their eyeballs and over their elbows. And that's what Oscar did."

"We tried something new tonight against Robertson," said Auerbach with a sad smile. "I told my boys to stretch their fingers out wide, with their hands way up on defense, figuring every little bit helps. But you know what Oscar did? He shot through their fingers."

Lucas was saying that Robertson is the only player he has ever seen who can get a good shot off anytime he wanted to. "Oscar has such absolute control of the ball and of his body that he can put a defender where he wants to with a fake, and if he can't, he's so strong that he can muscle his way by him. Even if a big man covers him under the basket, he can get him going up and down with head and shoulder fakes so that Oscar is finally going up while the other guy's coming back down, and that's all there is to it. If Oscar ever really sets out to see how many points he could score in a single game, there's no telling how high he can go."

Robertson was asked if he would ever want to score 65 or 75 points in a game. "That will just never happen," he said, somewhat disgusted at the thought. "Never. What would that possibly prove?"

With the victory over the Celtics, the Royals were now 4½ games behind in second place. The next day was an off day. There was more good news. The Eastern Division team was named for the NBA All-Star game in Boston on January 14. Robertson, Lucas and Embry were selected from the Royals. It would be Robertson's fourth straight All-Star game.

On December 29 the Royals were still home and beat the Knicks, 105-99. Robertson scored 29 points on 8 of 19 from the floor and 13 of 13 from the free-throw line. He did this despite a jammed and swollen middle finger on his shooting hand suffered in the Celtic game.

Robertson had a chance to break Bill Sharman's all-time free-throw record of 56 straight. He now had 36 in a row. But his string ended in the next game. Robertson made five straight free throws against Detroit at Dayton, then missed. It gave him 41 in a row, a club record. The game itself, however, ended on a happier note for the Royals, who won, 112-111. Oscar had 32 points. It was also a good game for speedy Jay Arnette, who hustled for 12 points.

The Royals were on another winning streak of four games, but this one ended the following night in Philadelphia. The 76ers beat the Royals decisively, 132-110. Robertson had 27 points. Then it was four more wins in a row for Cincinnati as they beat New York, Baltimore and Philadelphia twice.

The third game in the string was against Philadelphia at Columbus, Ohio. It was a triumphant return for Jerry Lucas, who, in a game there during preseason play, had been humiliated in the worst game he could ever remember playing. When he was introduced just before this game, Lucas received another standing ovation from the crowd of 6,963. Among the spectators in the state Capitol was Governor James Rhodes. Lucas had been a "confused, raw rookie," as one reporter described him in September. Now they saw an increasingly polished, confident professional, a player living up to his superstar days as a collegian.

Lucas opened the game with a jump shot. He went on to score a total of 23 points and grabbed 14 rebounds. He made 8 of 12 from the field. And he held the 76ers' Chet Walker to just three field goals. Robertson had 26 points and also pulled down 14 rebounds. The Royals won, 130-110.

The Royals had now won 8 of their last 9 games, 12 of their last 14 and 19 of their last 24. The Celtics, meanwhile, had lost three straight road games—to Los Angeles on consecutive nights, then to San Francisco. The Royals were now just 1½ games behind the Celtics, and the two clubs would meet at Boston Gardens on Friday night, January 10. For the first time since 1957 the Celtics were being seriously challenged.

Nineteen fifty-seven was the year Russell sustained an injury and was unable to play in the final two playoff games against St. Louis. It was the only time the Celtics had lost the championship since Russell joined them. Now Russell was ailing again, with a thigh injury, and did not play in those three losing games on the coast. But he would be in the lineup against the Royals.

When the Royals arrived in Boston, reporters clamored around McMahon. Boston was brimming for the game. One newspaper carried a full-page cartoon of Oscar and bannered it with IT'S OSCAR - TIME AGAIN.

Boston led at the half, 49-48. Then Boston scored 8 straight points. Robertson made a free throw. Then the Celtics scored 6 straight points and led, 63-49. In the third period the Celtics outscored Cincinnati, 32-17, with Sam Jones hitting on five straight long jump shots. The Celtics won, 109-92. Sam Jones was high scorer for Boston with 28 points, followed by Havlicek with 23 and Heinsohn with 21. Bill Russell, showing little effects of a sore thigh, had 32 rebounds and 12 points.

Robertson was high scorer in the game with 32 points, but it was not a particularly good game for him. He seemed to force his offense and was persistent about driving against Russell, but with little success. Only Lucas played up to his capabilities, scoring 22 points and getting 15 rebounds. Afterward, McMahon said quietly, "I didn't get anything out of three of my first five." Twyman had scored 7 points with but 2 rebounds, Embry had 7 points and 6 rebounds, Bockhorn had 6 points. Hawkins, the first forward substitute, performed adequately with 10 points.

Now the Royals had dropped 2½ games behind the league

leaders. Oscar, however, did have something to celebrate that day. In Cincinnati, Yvonne had given birth to their second daughter, Tia Elaine.

The Royals returned home to play Detroit two nights later. Meanwhile, the Celtics were beaten by the 76ers. The Royals then solidly whipped the Pistons, 120-88, and again trailed Boston by 1½ games. They would have to wait, however, to resume the chase. It was now the All-Star-game break.

14

It took Robertson, Embry and Lucas thirty-two hours to travel from Cincinnati to Boston for the All-Star game. It may have been the longest trip east of the Mississippi since the Cumberland Road was built. There was a fierce snowstorm in Boston on Monday, January 13, the day before the All-Star game. The Royal group took off from Cincinnati but the plane had to make a detour to Chicago because of impossible landing conditions in Boston. There was an eight-hour delay in Chicago's O'Hare Airport.

With the players were a few Cincinnati reporters and Steve Hoffman, the Royals' publicity man. They were soon joined by Bailey Howell, picked as an All-Star from the Detroit Pistons. Howell, too, had been in a plane that was detoured, and he provided some entertainment for an otherwise dreary contingent that kept checking watches, checking the airlines desk and wearily browsing and sniffing through the airport. Howell was concerned about whether the Pistons were paying his meal money during this delay.

"If the Pistons won't," said Robertson, straight-faced, "I'll see if we can get the league office to work something out for you."

This was particularly humorous—in a gallows sort of way—since the players had been battling with the league to squeeze out some nickels for a modest pension plan. For five years, the NBA players had been delayed, put off, told to hold on by the owners. But there was no pension plan.

("All we wanted," said Bill Russell, "was a contributory plan which amounted to $500 from the team and $500 from the player. It was a very modest start, but we felt it could develop . . . (but) in reply we received the swerve and the stall and the screws.")

Robertson was the player representative for the Royals and was strongly in favor of the pension plan. He did not like the haughty attitude of the owners. Robertson felt totally justified in evening things out in the relationship between owner and player, for it smacked too much of lord and serf.

"This is something that can't be overstressed, a player's years are very limited, and we have no benefits other than salary," he said. "A lot of owners think since they're paying you this salary, you owe your life to them. But here you have the American Football League, only three or four years old, and they have a player association and are working on a pension plan."

The player representatives, including stars like Tom Heinsohn—who was also the president of their union, the National Basketball Players' Association—and Jerry West and Bob Pettit, had discussed the possibility of striking before the All-Star game if the owners still procrastinated about a pension plan. Now, however, the Royals and Howell were more concerned about getting out of that Chicago airport than striking or even playing in Boston. Robertson always found these delays the hardest part of traveling. Because of the snowstorm, all flights to Boston had been canceled. Finally, they were able to make connections to fly to Washington. From there they would get a train to Boston. So the rumpled bunch landed in Washington at 1:30 A.M. Tuesday. They went to a nearby hotel. About the time they were falling asleep, the desk was ringing them. They were up at five-thirty to catch the six-thirty train to Boston.

At 3:40 P.M. the conductor called that the train would enter the Boston station in twenty minutes. A howl from a certain knot of people startled the other passengers in the car. It was the end of a thirty-two-hour journey.

The basketball group, blurry in the knee and fuzzy in the head, staggered off the train into snow-whipped Boston. They had a game to play in five hours, at 9 P.M. And what took place in the locker room before the game, as it turned out, was as suspenseful as the previous trip and more dramatic than the upcoming game.

A capacity crowd of nearly 14,000 was expected, as well as a national television audience. But the twenty players huddled in the Eastern All-Stars dressing room for the strike vote. There was about this whole thing a tremor of hysteria. The blizzard had held up some of the crowd and some of the owners. The television people were stoking their dyspepsia. The first-year NBA commissioner, Walter Kennedy, was trying to bring the owners and players together. (And he did not want any snags with his new television deal for the league.) Some of the superstars were a bit shaky about their actions, afraid to alienate their owners. According to Bill Russell, there was a superstar who usually spoke articulately but who stuttered, "W-w-w-ell, we h-h-ave t-to-understand th-th-their p-p-point."

"Shut up," someone said.

Robertson was prepared to sit and wait a long time—he had just experienced thirty-two hours of that sort of training. The players voted 11-9 to play. Another vote was taken. This time it was 11-9 to strike.

At 8:30 p.m., half an hour before gametime, Kennedy, after talking with a few owners, came into the locker room and promised the players that satisfactory agreement would be worked out in the league meetings in May. They took his word, and Kennedy later made good on it.

The players came on the court at 8:55 p.m. Robertson was adamant about a change in owner-player relationships. Two years later, in 1966, he would take over Heinsohn's role as president of the Players' Association, which would gain him the respect and admiration of the players off the court as well as on. The players voted him in again for several years following. What they respected most was that he would put his impressive name and reputation on the line for issues like pension plans and insurance policies, monetary issues that made little difference to one in his $100,000-a-year bracket. But it was the fringe players, the guys barely making five figures, that reaped the advantage.

"He has done wonders for us," said Bud Olsen, who would soon leave the Royals and then shift from team to team for a few years. "He helped better the pension plan, got us more meal money on the road, from $7 a day to $16, and worked to get family-plan insurance programs. He upgraded the whole league. And he sure didn't have to do it for himself. He did it for the small man like me. Now every time I see him I thank him. I also kid him. I'll say to him, 'Well, Oz, what are you going to do for us this year?'"

Larry Fleisher, lawyer for the Players' Association, said about Robertson, "He is the most forceful and strongest leader in the union. We got more accomplished since he has been president than in all of the previous fifteen years. Maybe the biggest thing he has done is to establish collective bargaining with the owners. Now the players were able to say no to people who were once unapproachable."

Besides being forceful, Robertson brings intelligence and insight to the position, which are the qualities that also contribute to his success as a basketball player. Walter Paul, president of Queen Dity Barrel Co. in Cincinnati, was one of Robertson's college "sponsors." He believed that Robertson could have been an A student at Cincinnati had it not been for the demands of basketball.

"Oscar's recall is almost unbelievable," Paul said. "He can recite just about every principle of economics he has learned. I've never seen anyone read faster than he does and still digest the material."

And Robertson's ability to measure people and situations is as good or better than it was as a senior in high school. At that time the Attucks assistant principal told George Smith, then recruiting Oscar, "Oscar never will be a behavior problem. He has a nice way of avoiding bad elements. He has a knack for sizing up people who are in the rackets and he avoids them like poison."

Yvonne, Oscar's wife, said, "Oscar respects honesty in a person above everything else. He hates phonies. He has had a lot of experience with phonies, as anyone in the public eye will." Now, before the All-Star game in Boston, he trusted the roundish, baldish, bright-eyed new commissioner and so, somewhat appeased, Robertson trotted onto the court. The turmoil of business and money faded into the shouting crowd and the lighted court. Robertson was no longer a financier. He was a basketball player.

Like all great athletes, Robertson thrives on challenges. It is a cliché that has been whittled to the core, but it is nonetheless true. And Robertson exemplifies it. He has, as McMahon said, "tremendous pride." "The tougher the competition," Robertson has said, "the more I put out."

It has been that way with Robertson ever since he could remember. It is what drove him to practice so hard when he was a youngster so that he could come back to the Dust Bowl in Indianapolis to play with the bigger boys who had earlier sent him packing. It was that way in other sports, too. When he was in college, for example, one evening a friend took him to a recreation center in Cincinnati to play table tennis. The friend, Harold Trotter, was an accomplished table-tennis player. Robertson was a novice. "He knew he was going to beat me," recalled Robertson. "But I wasn't going to let him. I played him almost all night until I beat him."

It is this force within him that enflames his bile on the court. "Let's say I'm playing against somebody and he blocks my shot," said Robertson. "I say to myself, 'You won't do it again.' I figure the next time I'll know how he'll react and be ready for him." And it was this quality of pride that has made Robertson take care of his talents and body, as his mother had advised when his was just a boy, and to take such precautions as wearing dark glasses in midwinter to keep the wind from hurting his eyes.

Oscar wants to be the best wherever he is, under whatever circumstances. Once, on an August day, he went to a gym in Cincinnati for a workout. He had just returned from a vacation in Europe and had not touched a basketball in

several weeks. Coincidentally, Jack Twyman, Connie Dierking, Tom Thacker, Wayne Embry and some other players
were also there. They were involved in choose-up games. Oscar joined in.

"He looked a little soft," recalled one spectator. "He
looked liked he had a roll around his waist and a roll under
his chin. He looked like he hadn't played in a year. He looked
like a bullfrog, in fact—unk-unk-unk."

Gary Gray, a hopeful Royal rookie, was also playing.
Gray had been working himself into top shape for the challenge ahead. This afternoon he was put on Robertson. An
hour later he was gasping. Gray recalled, "I couldn't say I
guarded Oscar. I kind of watched him."

There was a night, years later, when Robertson's competitive zeal was demonstrated with clarity and force. It was
the night in Madison Square Garden when Bill Bradley—
like Oscar one of the most celebrated college players in
history—upon his return from two years of study in England
and the signing of a half-million-dollar contract, was to play
for the Knicks. Bradley had been termed by some "The
White O."

Robertson was playing with a heavily taped thigh, but
from the opening tipoff he was out to show the Garden crowd
that there was only one O, white or black.

He picked up the slim newcomer at midcourt and played
him eyelash-to-eyelash throughout the first half. He hounded
Bradley, pursued him, talked to him, never let him get a crack
of daylight. Once, when the ball was going toward the hoop
and eyes had been diverted from this gluey pair, Robertson crouched in front of Bradley at midcourt and half-threw
a left jab into his stomach, as if to say that even when the
ball was not nearby, Robertson was.

At the half, Bradley had managed to get off only two shots,

153

a 20-foot jumper and—the only time he was able to free himself from Robertson—a jump shot at the free-throw line. Both missed. Bradley did little more the second half. By then, Robertson was guarding someone else.

One of Robertson's earliest personal challenges in the NBA came after his sixth game in his rookie year. One night, Tom Gola of Philadelphia held Robertson to 14 points. "I had a bad ankle," said Robertson, "but that's no excuse. Gola just outsmarted me."

Gola had watched Robertson on television. He saw that Robertson was dribbling too much. "I could see him lining up his shots off the dribble," said Gola. So Robertson had but three field goals and his lowest point total since his college days, when Houston held him to 13.

"He's not a true backcourtman yet," said Neil Johnston, Gola's teammate. "He hasn't got the outside shot to keep you honest. We sag on him and try to beat him inside."

Robertson took this all in. When the Royals met the Warriors two weeks later, Robertson's adrenaline gurgled. He scored 44 points, got 15 rebounds and the Royals won, 124-115.

For Oscar, then, a big game does not necessarily have to be a championship confrontation, or a contest against the Celtics. It could be a game in a town he has never before played in. The challenge is never-ending.

"You always know the town Oscar has never played in," said McMahon, years later. "I remember when Atlanta was to open their first season. The Royals were the first opponents. I told people, 'Watch this Oscar.' I was right. He killed them. Same thing happened at the Astrodome in the first NBA game there. And Oscar is always great—greater than usual, I should say—on nationally televised games. If I was a betting man, that's the kind of inside dope I'd be looking for."

Basically, the NBA's East-West All-Star game was, for Robertson, little different from, say, the high school all-star games between the Indiana and Kentucky standouts. It was a show of shows and from it would be determined the star of stars. Oscar wanted to be center stage, just as the other nineteen players in the game desired to be, though probably not as fervently.

Robertson, of course, has been selected to play in every All-Star game since he entered the NBA. And it is no coincidence that in his first nine years the team Oscar played for won eight times; he was with the winner his first six times—this despite Cincinnati moving from the Western Division to the Eastern in 1963 (the significance here being that in the first two years Chamberlain and Russell were both on the East team when Robertson was with the West).

Robertson had been a sensation in three previous All-Star games. He had the phenomenal achievement of being the game's Most Valuable Player in his rookie year. If there had been any doubts about just how good Robertson was, he squelched them that night in Syracuse as the West won, 153-131. Robertson scored 23 points, pulled down 9 rebounds and, most sensationally, he had much of the crowd of 8,016 on its feet most of the night as he penetrated and picked up 14 assists, breaking Bob Cousy's All-Star-game assists record by one. The following two years he was runner-up as Most Valuable Player, scoring 26 and 21 points.

The game this night in Boston lacked the spark, the flavor of the previous games. It was due to two factors: travel fatigue, since most of the players—as those in the Royals' group—had spent hours getting there because of the blizzard; and absorption with the pension plan. Those players who were in Boston hardly sat around resting. They scampered about in pursuit of their retirement security.

The East was a slight favorite, particularly since the starting team of Russell, Heinsohn, Sam Jones, Lucas and Robertson were averaging 121 points. The first team for the West was Pettit, Baylor, West, Rodgers and Bellamy (who was playing ahead of Chamberlain because only he and Russell were unanimous picks by the sportswriters).

For the first 21 minutes the teams clomped back and forth on the court as though they had forgotten to take off their snowshoes. Then the East, led by Robertson, spurted with an 11-2 advantage and took a 56-50 halftime lead. They increased it in the second half, and only once was there a hint of the game getting tingly. West, scoring on his superb long jumper, brought the West to within 5, 96-91, in the last period. But Robertson came back with two quick baskets and the matter was virtually decided.

Robertson scored 26 points—no one else in the game had over 19. Robertson had 8 assists, three more than anyone else. He also had 14 rebounds, a fantastic number for a guard, and only Russell (naturally) and Chamberlain (naturally) and Pettit (naturally) had more. Before the game, Len Chappell of the Knicks, playing in his first All-Star game, expressed concern to an experienced teammate. "I was worried," recalled Chappell, "that the players represented teams with different patterns and there would be confusion on the court. This one player told me, 'Don't worry about patterns if Oscar is there. He knows every one of them and he'll put them all together.' He did. Every time I was open he hit me with a pass, and when I wasn't, he found another man. He took everybody's system and put it into one working pattern."

There was no contest for Most Valuable Player in the game. Of the forty-three sportswriters' ballots, 4½ votes went to Hal Greer, 5 to Russell and 33½ to Robertson.

Before returning home to Cincinnati, Robertson and Embry did some shopping in Boston the morning following the game. Among Oscar's purchases was a rock album for Yvonne. It was by Lockjaw Davis and entitled "I Only Have Eyes For You." Covering much of the album were two large eyes shaped like Big O's.

15

Robertson returned home from Boston with his MVP trophy on the same day that Yvonne returned home from the hospital with five-day-old Tia Elaine. It was a good day.

The Robertsons lived in a two-story seven-room Tudor house at the end of a cul-de-sac on Eaton Lane. It was in the area called Avondale, wooded, upper-middle class, quiet. In the macadam driveway sat a white Cadillac. Nailed to the garage was a backboard and orange-rim basket with corded net; it was the only such apparatus on Eaton Lane. When Robertson bought the house the neighborhood was integrated. In following years it became all-Negro.

Before he purchased the house, there had been rumors that he wanted to move into an all-white neighborhood. In later years he would hear comments that he planned to move.

But he hastened to alleviate the fears of lily-white realtors and homeowners. "Every once in a while a story gets out that we're about to move into a white neighborhood," he said. "I believe the word that's always used is 'exclusive.' But I have no intention of living where I'm not wanted." He also did not want to create undue hardships for his children. "In this world there's so little to be happy about, so why make your life unbearable just to prove a point." When the children grew older and more room was needed, the Robertsons did search for a new house. "We're looking in the same neighborhood," he said, "because we like it here."

Robertson, though, did eventually get involved in race relations in the neighborhood. "They were bussing kids from our neighborhood to another school," he said. "But the white people didn't want their kids bussed into our neighborhood. This was the first time I ever got interested in this stuff. 'What's wrong with our school?' I asked them."

Robertson had looked forward to coming home; he always did after road trips, but now even more so. He had called Yvonne at the hospital several times a day—at the airport in Chicago when he and the others were stranded for eight hours, and again several times from Boston. Oscar has an uncommon respect for his wife, and when one talks about him with people he deals with, teammates, friends and business associates, they are unanimous in the conviction that Yvonne has greatly influenced his life.

"I roomed with Oscar for six years on the road," said Embry, "and I still feel as though I don't know him. I think only two people really do, his mother and his wife. Yvonne is very, very intelligent and sensitive and sensible. Mature. She's older than him, too. How much older? Well, I'd rather not get into that. Anyway, it seems there is a sort of mutual admiration there. A great deal of respect for each other."

"Before meeting her," said another friend who has known

Robertson for several years, "he was extremely moody and distant, not very approachable. Steve Hoffman had problems when Robertson joined the Royals. "He almost drove me to the brink," said Hoffman. "It was murder to get him to do an interview. He always seemed afraid that people were out to get as much as they could from him, without giving anything in return. But that's changed now. He's been great. Why, you can even call him at home now to tape an interview."

Jerry West played with Robertson on the U.S. team in the Pan-American games in 1959, and was co-captain with him on the Olympic team in Rome the following fall, just a few months after the Robertsons were married. "It's amazing how Oscar grew up in the last year," said West after the Olympics. "He's become a different ballplayer. He's quieter and steadier, and I've got an idea his marriage helped."

Others noticed that, though Oscar continued to play with customary intensity, he also had less fits of pique on the court, toward himself and toward teammates.

"Yvonne," wrote another Robertson observer, "gradually convinced him that life wasn't all bad; that there were broad-minded people in the world as well as bigots, and that a Negro, like anyone else, can expect to get as much out of life as he was willing to put in."

Yvonne Robertson is a well-rounded woman, physically and intellectually. She has delicate facial features and a soft café-au-lait complexion. A cultured woman, she plays piano "well enough to teach children" and is a respectable artist. ("No, I haven't done a sketch of Oscar," she says with a smile. "He's not still long enough.") She has whetted Oscar's appetite for the arts—though he does not like to admit it, especially to her. "Just give me those cowboy and Indian movies, the heck with operas," he teases her. His interest in reading was surely cultivated by her. He has read almost everything by Ayn Rand, who writes staunchly that one must live by high and unwavering principles and a firm conviction of individualism.

"Ayn Rand stimulates me," he said. "What she writes about everyday life seems to work out for me just the way she says it will." Robertson empathizes with her heroic characters who attain excellence despite the Philistine world around them.

In *The Fountainhead* protagonist Howard Roark says:

> Throughout the centuries there were men who took first steps down new roads armed with nothing but their own vision. Their goals differed, but they all had this in common: That the step was first, the road new, the vision unborrowed, and the response they received —hatred. The great creators—the thinkers, the artists, the scientists, the inventors—the thinkers, the men of their time. . . The creator lives for his work.

Robertson continues to believe that fans often hope the star athlete fails. For the star athlete is a "superman" of sorts. He has put together long training and physical and mental development, overcome pressures and demands, to excel— something most fans never attain and can only appreciate vicariously. When a star athlete fails, the spectator becomes equal to the "superman." He sees that both are fallible. The athlete is unable to reason this out. He only feels it— and resents it. But Yvonne's level-headed influence has made Oscar understand this, even if only on a subconscious level.

Oscar and Yvonne Crittenden, then a first-grade schoolteacher, met at a dance at the YMCA on the UC campus when Robertson was an upper-classman. Robertson and a friend were there stag. Oscar was too shy to approach Yvonne alone, so he solicited his friend to get her phone number. What happened afterward has become a family joke that

Oscar enjoys with downcast eyes. "When he called me," said Yvonne, "we double-dated. And he spent the whole night talking to his friend."

When they were married, Yvonne was teaching in Cincinnati. Her six-year-old pupils would ask, "Mrs. Oscar Robertson, may I sharpen my pencil?" "Mrs. Oscar Robertson, may I go to the restroom?"

The Robertsons did many things together. Oscar would be hunched over the kitchen table helping Yvonne with her school records, and she in turn would accompany him on such nocturnal excursions as when Robertson and a few others, helping to recruit for UC, went to the airport at two in the morning to meet George Wilson, then the star center at Marshall High School in Chicago. Yvonne and Oscar like music and spent long hours listening to their hi-fi in the rec room enjoying Lockjaw Davis, Fats Domino, Dizzy Gillespie, Oscar Peterson and Cannonball Adderley. And they danced together, with Oscar delighting in doing new dance steps like the "slop" and the "horse." Inevitably, they also spent a certain portion of their time doing what Oscar enjoys with relish—television-viewing.

Early in their marriage, Robertson cultivated a mustache. "He acted as if he were so proud of it," she said. "I'm sure he was putting on a show just because he knew I didn't like the mustache." The black caterpillar over the lip soon came off.

Over the years, Robertson had developed a weight problem. Some of it begins at home, where Yvonne is an accomplished cook. And both have grown increasingly careful of sumptuous dinners.

"Steak and roast beef used to be his favorites," said Yvonne. "Now he leans toward soul food . . . beans, pinto and black mostly, and lots of pork." Though Yvonne has a passion for Chinese food, Oscar has a frostier attitude toward those dishes. "Oscar," she said, "wants something with more sustenance." She laughed. "As far as he's concerned, Chinese food might make a good appetizer."

As he does in hotel rooms on the road, Robertson often handles a basketball at home, flicking it back and forth to practice fingertip control, swinging it around his body. Yvonne has watched this ritual with enchantment. "It has to do with the touch," she says. "The touch of the ball and the sensitivity of the ball in his hands. There's something almost mystical about the way he talks about it."

"I don't know if I can explain it myself," said Robertson. "It's just a feeling I get with the ball that makes me think I can handle it. Maybe it gets my muscles flexed out. The feel of the ball is in the fingertips. I know that whenever my fingers are cool I don't feel the ball very well."

Yvonne was not a great basketball fan before meeting Oscar, but she has come to understand and appreciate the game. She attends many Royal home games and sits with the other players' wives at courtside, usually with Shana and Tia, who have come to delight in the atmosphere of the event, particularly the boxes of popcorn at halftime. "They also loved to clap when a basket was made," said Yvonne, years later. "They'd clap for a basket by Oscar the same as a basket by another Royal—or by the other team! I soon broke them of *that* habit."

One element of a pro-basketball player's life that did take some getting used to was her husband's predilection for staying in bed. "Maybe he thinks he's not getting enough sleep," said Yvonne. "Maybe all pro-basketball players are tired all the time."

Or maybe it was an excuse so he wouldn't have to fix a leaky faucet.

16

The pursuit of the Celtics was resumed. The Royals were confident they would beat the Celtics, but they would need more help from the other clubs.

The Royals returned to action after the All-Star break with élan, and success. At home against the Lakers, Cincinnati won, 108-95. Robertson had 32 points. Lucas scored his pro career high of 29 points. But the brightest light for the Royals was Arlen Bockhorn, the gritty guard. He held Jerry West to 8 points. West made only 3 of 18 field-goal attempts. "Everywhere I went," lamented West afterward, "there was that damn Bockhorn in front of me."

The Hawks came to town two nights later for the first of two games with Cincy. The Hawks were in second place in the Western Division, three games behind the Lakers. The

Laker-Hawk Western Division battle of the previous year was a typical case of home-court advantage. In the best-of-seven series, Los Angeles won the first two games, which were played in Los Angeles. St. Louis won the next two games, which were played in St. Louis. Los Angeles won the fifth game, in Los Angeles. St. Louis won the sixth game, in St. Louis. And with the series tied, 3-3, all home teams being victorious, the teams traveled back to Los Angeles, where Los Angeles won the seventh and deciding game. With this kind of history, the Hawks were hungry to pass the Lakers in the standings, and stay there.

At the end of the third quarter the Royals led the Hawks, 95-93, but both Robertson and Lucas had accumulated four fouls. Both were on the bench as the fourth quarter opened. The importance of this star pair was never more in evidence. The Hawks bounded away to a 13-2 advantage in the quarter. The stars returned, and Robertson scored 9 of the Royals next 11 points as they rushed to make up the difference. It was 116-108, St. Louis, with 3:28 left in the game. The Royals kept pushing and Lucas tipped in a basket to tie the score with a minute left. Then Cliff Hagan was fouled and hit a free throw—56 seconds left. The Hawks pressed. Robertson tried to dribble through but had the ball stolen by Wilkens, who passed to Pettit. Lucas blocked Pettit's shot. The Royals hurried downcourt with a three-on-one fast break, but Chico Vaughn stole the ball from Twyman and passed to Wilkens, who was fouled intentionally by Bockhorn to prevent a layup. Wilkens made both free throws and the Hawks led by 3 with 8 seconds to go. Bockhorn made a final shot. Not enough. Hawks, 121-120. Though Robertson had to sit out part of the game and had to be careful not to pick up two more fouls, he wound up with 40 points, exactly a third of his team's points.

In St. Louis the next night, the Royals again had to contend with the fierce Hawks and their equally ferocious fans. Robertson was hot from the beginning, scoring on several consecutive baskets against Wilkens. At 6-1, 185, Wilkens had to rely on tenacity and speed—and help from team-mates—to try to stop Robertson. Robertson relied on his muscle, including his trusty forearm. Near the end of the first quarter, Robertson, pounding the ball, worked his way relentlessly under the basket for a short shot and missed, but Wilkens was called for a foul and blew up. Wilkens screamed that Robertson was using his arm illegally. Now a technical foul was called on Wilkens. Robertson sank the technical foul shot as well as the two free throws awarded him on the missed shot and the Royals led, 27-26.

Robertson never denies that he uses strong-arm tactics. "All that talk about sportsmanship is fine," said Robertson. "But you don't get paid for it. You get paid for putting the ball in the basket. And for winning. So you have to do every-thing you can to accomplish those things."

It was 65-all at the half, but the Hawks pulled away to lead by 18 in the fourth quarter and finally won, 114-109. Wil-kens had little success with Robertson, who scored 44 points, hitting on 14 of 21 shots from the floor. The Royals had now lost two straight. Meanwhile, the Celtics had won four straight since the All-Star-game break.

On January 21 the Royals played the Knicks in Madison Square Garden. Before the game, McMahon gathered the players in the locker room and blasted the team because he thought they were letting down. He knew, though, that in a long season there must be some low physical and mental points. His face was florid but his voice even. "It's the first time this team has not been giving a good effort," he said. "I want it to stop."

Though players and coaches are schooled in the cliché that they "play 'em one at a time," McMahon was nonetheless looking one night ahead to the game against Boston at Cincinnati. The Knicks could conceivably beat the Royals but it was unlikely. However, McMahon feared a continued disintegration. A loss to the Knicks would hardly give his club momentum for Boston. And McMahon's clubhouse talk worked. The Royals beat the Knicks, 139-121, with Robertson getting 31 points. And the next night they beat the Celtics solidly, 109-92. But not before a bit of a fright.

At the outset of the third quarter the Royals had a 21-point lead. And with 9:01 left in the game they were coasting, 63-49, so McMahon thought he could safely rest Robertson. He tried. But when the Celtics came to within 8 points, 72-64, Robertson was rushed back in with 4:28 left. He scored 7 straight points to ease the tension and finished with 38 points. The Celtics' season record now stood at 32-11. The Royals were 33-17, 2½ games behind.

The Royals, perhaps too high now, lost two straight, to Philadelphia and Baltimore. On January 30 they traveled to Detroit, where they would play New York in the first game of a doubleheader. And there they began the most successful single period in Royal history. They were to win twelve straight games. It did not start out brightly, however, but what seemed portentous at the time actually became a blessing. In a scramble for a loose ball, Bockhorn injured his knee. Smith took over and played so well the rest of the regular season that he remained in the lineup, even when Bockhorn was healthy again.

"That was my best move of the season, keeping Odie in the starting lineup," McMahon said years later. "Odie's a great complement to Oscar. And he's a terrific shot. Oscar penetrates, Odie stays back. The other team never gets an uncontested fast break when Odie's in the game."

The Royals beat New York that night in Detroit, 133-110, with Smith scoring 14 points. Twyman was high scorer with

29 points. Robertson had 28, but most remarkable was his 18 assists. It broke the Cobo Hall assists record and was one of many assist records Robertson would establish, the most important being the career record of 6,949 held by Cousy. Robertson would break it five years later, on February 16, 1969. Andy Cox, who was the Royals' publicity director then, had been anticipating the record-breaking event for some time and had tried to do something special. He hit upon a brainstorm. Why not get a giant spoon to present to the "Greatest Feeder of All Time"?

Cox wanted an object 10 feet tall. It was ordered. But there was a mixup with the Midwest manufacturer, so on the day Robertson broke the record all Cox could do was have the game stopped in Cincinnati Gardens and the game ball presented to Oscar. It was a crushing blow to Cox, but Oscar seemed as unconcerned about not getting the spoon as he was about the record. In the locker room, Robertson was asked how he felt about receiving the game ball. "Tired," he said. "We had a game last night in Chicago, and we got in at four in the morning. Getting the ball gave me a chance to rest." Prodded, Robertson admitted he was proud of the accomplishment.

The achievement was even more noteworthy in that Cousy established the mark after thirteen seasons. Robertson broke the record in his ninth NBA year.

After beating the Knicks to start that twelve-game winning streak, the Royals played the Bullets the next night, Friday, January 31, in Dayton. Robertson did not break any assist records; all he did was score 35 points and pull down 17 rebounds in the win.

They next played Boston, and Robertson had one of his greatest shooting nights. He had scored 42 points with 7 seconds left in the game, but the score was tied, 111-111.

And for all his heroics over the previous 47 minutes and 53 seconds, Robertson almost became the goat of the game. He threw an in-bounds pass directly into the hands of John Havlicek. Havlicek missed the short shot, got his own rebound and missed again. In the 5-minute overtime period, Boston hustled out to a 117-112 lead, with Robertson getting the lone Royal point. Then Oscar scored 5 more. Amazingly, the Royals held the Celtics scoreless in the final 3 minutes. The Royals won, 119-117, on Lucas's two free throws with 11 seconds left. Oscar scored 48 points and Lucas 34. But the Royals were still in second place, three games down.

The Royals then beat Los Angeles in Cincinnati in their twenty-fourth home game of the season. The Royals had now drawn 162,261 fans, already surpassing last season's figure of 137,739. They still had nine home games left to break the record of 194,017 set in Robertson's rookie year.

Another home crowd of over 10,000 watched the Royals extend their winning streak to five with a 126-114 win over Philadelphia. The game had been close at the outset until Robertson got angry. The 76ers double- and triple-teamed Oscar with the maximum of body bumps and elbow jabs. The most egregious offender was Ben Warley. Robertson flared up and he and Warley squared off in the best of tin-type poses of a bare-knuckle era. No punches were thrown. But Oscar got hot with his shooting hand, as well as his temper. In the fourth quarter, Warley came busting out of nowhere to send Robertson sprawling, but Robertson managed to take Warley with him. It was Warley's sixth foul and he left with bruised buttocks, and a bruised ego: Robertson had scored 42 points in the game.

Cincinnati's win at Baltimore was its sixth straight and tied a club record. Baltimore had come to within 5 points with 2 minutes left in the game, but Robertson's six free throws saved the victory.

Win number seven, 135-107, over Detroit, with a highlight not only for the Royals, who broke the club record, but for Odie Smith, who scored his career high of 23 points.

NBA statistics that came out the next day showed that Robertson was leading the league in scoring with a 30.5 average, was tops in assists with 627, the leader in field-goal percentage with .524 and among the leaders in total rebounds.

The eighth-straight win was against Detroit again. Smith, hitting 16 points, making few mistakes and hustling as if for his life, was again an important cog. The Royals next beat New York at home and, the next night, February 15, beat the Knicks at New York. In that one the Royals came close to having their streak snapped. They were behind, 71-59, at the half but came back to tie it, 118-118. Robertson hit a jumper to send them into the lead and they never trailed again.

In their third straight game in as many nights, the Royals whipped the 76ers in Cincinnati, then beat San Francisco, 129-113, at Cleveland for their twelfth straight.

It was one of the largest turnouts for a basketball game in the history of the Cleveland Arena, 11,595. The starting players were introduced one by one and trotted onto the floor. Robertson limped on. He had been a doubtful starter, having pulled a thigh muscle the game before. But he wanted to play, had to play. Every game was important now. Like most players in the NBA, Robertson will allow no injury short of broken legs to keep him out of the lineup. Once, he was incensed over a Boston newspaper story that intimated he was not playing when he could have. The headline read IS OSCAR REALLY HURT?

"I feel sorry for the guy who wrote that story," said Oscar, with little pity in his voice. "He doesn't know, and the fans usually don't know, that you're often playing with hamstrings aching, and tendons in your hands aching, and you're wondering if you can even go another step on the court, and your stomach is upset from a bad meal on the road and your head's fuzzy from a lousy night sleeping. But there's no sitting out."

When the whistle blew in Cleveland, neither the fans nor the Warriors could have guessed the pain Robertson was in. They probably would not have believed it, anyway. He scored 45 points.

The Royals not only had been winning, they had been winning with decisiveness. Only once in the last twelve games had the outcome been in doubt in the final minutes. That was against the Knicks, and Robertson had put a stop to that business quickly. The Royals were confident now as never before. The team was very much a unit; there is no string like victories to tie a team together. "We were all getting along tremendously," said Arnette after the season. "I never had so much fun playing on any team anywhere. It was probably the greatest thrill of my life."

Two nights later the Royals again played San Francisco, this time in Cincinnati. The Royals came onto the court to the roar of the nearly filled house, an appreciation of their terrific spurt over their last twelve games. The game began with a mysterious omen. Coach Alex Hannum of San Francisco, apparently at his wit's end with Oscar—as were the rest of his coaching colleagues—was prepared to try anything, and he almost did. He started the game by putting Wayne Hightower on Robertson. Hightower was normally a forward or center, positions at which any normal red-blooded 6-foot-10 American boy belonged. But Hannum had sat and stewed in previous games as he watched Robertson simultaneously bull and finesse his two guards, 6-1 Al Attles and

6-foot Guy Rodgers. The Royals and Oscar seemed a bit shaken at first with the unusual setup of having gawky Hightower flap above Robertson, so they fell behind.

Things improved a bit at halftime. Robertson remained on the court for the presentation to him of a portable television set from Sohio service-station dealers who had conducted a contest for the fans' "Favorite Royal." Robertson gave a short but gracious speech of thanks that he had written himself, with the advice and counsel of Yvonne. This little gesture was a mark of the growing change in Oscar.

Many times Robertson had been given awards for popularity and excellence and achievement; rarely had he said much more than thank you. Sometimes he would just smile shyly and accept the award. Robertson never felt a responsibility or inclination to be "humble" or feign a token of gratitude. He was rarely if ever excited about such things. Robertson has a sense of proportion. He knows that the awards are simply so much hardware, though, of course, he does not object to receiving them. When he was in college, for instance, and had been winning awards all over the country and had been in and out of airplanes and buses and cabs and hotel rooms and banquet halls, he once sat slumped on a chair in his dormitory room and asked his coach, "Why don't they just send me that stuff."

"That little acceptance speech," said Jim Schottelkotte, "is an example of how Oscar was coming out of his shell. Once an interview with him was just nods, and yes and no. Now he can really be cooperative."

A local newspaper photographer had a similar view. The day after that San Francisco game he went to Robertson's home for a photographic story. He approached the house on Eaton Lane with trepidation. "The last time I took a picture of him was when he was still at UC. You couldn't get him to do anything, just about," said the photographer. "He seemed unsure of himself, as if he was afraid of making a mistake. And maybe a little put out, too. But now, why, he and his wife were as cooperative as they could be. It seems that his years as a pro have brought maturity not only as a performer but as a person."

In the end, of course, Hightower could not stick with Oscar, and as usual the Cincinnati guard got his points, 29 this time. But Hightower matched that figure and Chamberlain got 32 points. The Royals lost, 108-101. Their twelve-game winning string was snapped.

Now the Royals began a nine-game road trip. They reaped some vengeance on the Warriors two nights later in the Cow Palace, beating San Francisco, 101-93. Then they traveled to Los Angeles, where they beat the Lakers by 2 points the next night. Back up to San Francisco two nights later, February 25, and the Warriors won; back down to Los Angeles the next night and the Royals lost again, this time by 6 points.

From Los Angeles they flew to Scranton, Pennsylvania, where they beat Philadelphia by 2 points to break a two-game losing streak. Then on to Philadelphia, where the Royals beat the 76ers by 3 points. Lucas had 40 rebounds for a league high for the season. Coincidentally, it was Leap Year Day.

On the first night of March the Royals were in Baltimore. The Royals had been leading throughout the game, but near the end of the third quarter the Bullets made a surge, caught them and passed them. The Royals tied it, then, with 6:42 left in the third quarter, Robertson hit a jump shot and the Royals led, 68-66, and never again trailed. The game was another typical second-half spurt for Robertson. He scored 35 points in the game, 21 came in the second half, including

13 in the final quarter. After the game, Bullet coach Bob Leonard said, "Oscar just turns it off and on when he wants. He's fantastic."

In New York, Robertson had what was for him a rather mediocre game. He had the ball stolen from him a few times and threw some passes that landed in the hands of the Knicks. Yet he finished with 33 points. The Royals won, 117-108.

"The Knicks had nothing to match [Robertson's] scoring," wrote one newspaperman, "but plenty to match his mistakes."

An interesting sidelight to the game was the Tuesday night Garden crowd of nearly 5,000. Traditionally the bulk of Tuesday night fans are more interested in the point spread than in who actually wins or loses. It is a crowd bent on supplementing their workaday incomes with investments on the outcome of the basketball game. Bookmakers favored the Royals by 7½ points. With 3 seconds left in the game the Royals led by 7, 115-108. The game, for gamblers, was still in doubt. The Royals took the ball out and got it to Lucas, who lofted a long shot just before the buzzer sounded. The ball swished through the net for the final 2 points. Cincinnati backers stood and cheered with such élan one would have thought this was Cincinnati Gardens instead of Madison Square Garden and that the Royals had just won the NBA championship by 1 point.

The season series with the Knicks ended with the Royals having an 11-1 edge in games. The Royals had won 18 out of their last 21 games, yet they were still 2½ games out. Boston's record was 53-19, to Cincinnati's 51-22. But a big series was coming up. The Royals would meet the Celtics tomorrow night, March 4, in Boston, then again in Cincinnati the following evening.

Time was running out for the Royals. They had seven games left in the regular season, the Celtics had eight. The first game in this series was the Royals' ninth straight road game and, as Robertson said, "the dirty socks were piling up." Though road trips can sap a player's energy, the Royals seemed not to be affected. They had won six of eight and four in a row.

The Celtics, too, entered the game on a high note, having won six straight. In the last one, against Philadelphia the night before, they had soared to a 23-9 lead and never lost the lead. Now, against Cincinnati, the Celtics had fallen behind, 90-85, with a minute gone in the final period. But now the Celtics took advantage of their fast break, the finest in basketball. A fast break must have stanch rebounding or defensive work to get it into motion. And, of course, that is where Bill Russell excelled. He could block a shot or snatch a defensive rebound, whip the ball to either of the Jones boys or Havlicek and the Celtics were gone in a whoosh. This weapon helped the Celtics outscore Cincinnati, 22-5, the rest of the way. They won, 115-108, and moved 3½ games in front, virtually clinching their eighth straight Eastern Division title. Robertson had scored 34 points, tops in the game, with Twyman and Lucas each getting 20. Havlicek was high for Boston with 28.

The Royals rebounded the next night, beating Boston, 111-101, in their first home game in over two weeks. A crowd of 11,855 pushed season attendance over 200,000. Robertson scored 27 points and had 15 rebounds and 17 assists. Lucas was also superb, scoring 22 points and getting a like number of rebounds.

Cincinnati beat Baltimore the night after. But the Celtics beat Detroit the same night and duplicated it the following evening. The Royals had won 20 of their last 24 games but had gained only half a game on the Celtics in that time.

"It's frustrating," said McMahon. "It's a shame when the rest of the league can't beat Boston."

And so on March 10 the Royals traveled to play the Pistons, and Detroit came back from two straight losses to Boston to beat Cincinnati. The Royals were mathematically eliminated from finishing first. They could only tie, but that was a remote possibility. The thought that now they would have to settle for second-place money was galling. They would have to try to make it up in the playoffs.

"With any kind of normal help from the other teams," said McMahon, "this could have been our year to win everything."

Only the Royals had been able to beat the Celtics in a season series, taking 7 of 12.

Philadelphia was the team the Royals would meet in the semifinals of the Eastern Division best-of-five playoffs. The winner would meet the Celtics. The Royals and 76ers got their final tuneup against each other on March 12 in Cincinnati, the last regular-season game between the two. The Royals won, 128-111, at Cincinnati, and thereby took the season series 9 games to 3. Meanwhile, Boston was rolling over Detroit, 140-120, on the same night and Celtic coach Red Auerbach was lighting his traditional victory cigar on the bench a full 5 minutes before game's end.

Now victories and defeats meant nothing more to the Royals than pride, until the playoffs began. On the next-to-last game of the regular season they lost to St. Louis by 8 points. Robertson scored 48 points and had a total of 2,455 for the season, surpassing his previous season high of 2,435 in 1961-62. For St. Louis, however, this game and the one the next night, March 15, in Cincinnati were very important. They were battling with San Francisco for first place in the West. Now, after the victory over Cincinnati, the Hawks had a 45-33 record; San Francisco was 47-31. The Hawks had to win their two remaining games and the Warriors had to lose both of theirs for a first-place tie. But the Hawks couldn't bring it off. They lost to the Royals, 124-101. Robertson scored 25 points to close out the season with a 31.4 average for a club record. His total of 2,480 points was also a club record, as were his 3,562 minutes played over the season.

Robertson finished the season with a 31.4-per-game scoring average, the best of his career, but not by far. Robertson's yearly consistency may be unparalleled in sports history. In his previous three seasons he had averaged 30.5, 30.8 and 28.3. After 1964 he would average 30.4, 31.3, 30.5 and 29.2. In this season he was nearly 5 points per game behind Wilt Chamberlain.

Robertson also led the league in assists with 868, a 10.9-per-game average. It was the third time in his four seasons that he was first in the league in assists. He was the best free-throw shooter in the game, with an average of .853; well behind in second place was Jerry West with .832. Robertson was also again the top rebounding guard, with 783 rebounds, nearly 10 a game. He was seventh in the league in field-goal percentage with .483 while West was sixth with .484—they were the lone guards in the top ten.

The Royals finished with a 55-25 record, their best ever, and the Celtics, with still two games left, would finish at 59-21, one victory short of the all-time number of games won in a single season, held by the Celtics of 1961-62. But the Bullets prevented Boston from tying the record by winning at Baltimore on the final day of the season.

Strange how the Royals could get within five games of that record and still not win the division championship.

17

Both benches were emptied and there was an angry swirl of 76er and Royal players on the court of Cincinnati Gardens; dukes were up, chests out, teeth bared. No punches were thrown. This was just before the half of their first playoff game. And it set the stage for the five-game series.

Before the series, McMahon had felt that the 76ers had an offensive advantage over the Royals while Cincinnati had stronger rebounding. Star shooter for Philadelphia was Hal Greer, who had averaged 22.3 for the season. When he was hot from outside he was nearly unstoppable. The 76ers had six other players who averaged in double figures, including forward Chet Walker at 17.3 and center Johnny Kerr at 16.8. Kerr was also formidable in other areas. He was considered one of the game's best pivot men, with a combination of experience, speed, passing skill, shooting and brains.

Philadelphia, however, was plagued by injuries and for the last month had played only seven men—Greer, Kerr, reserve center Connie Dierking, Warley, Walker and guards Paul Neumann and Al Bianchi. But now guard Dave Gambee was ready for the playoffs after having suffered a broken foot; guard Larry Costello, who also had a broken foot, was back; so was forward Lee Shaffer, who had an injured knee.

For Cincinnati, only Odie Smith was seriously hurt. He had sprained an ankle in the next-to-last game of the season against St. Louis, so Arlen Bockhorn had taken over again as starting guard with Robertson. But as long as they did not need a wheelchair, all players would be in uniform for the playoffs. They knew that if they made the divisional playoffs they would split at least $10,000 from that and then, if they won the division playoffs, would split maybe $20,000 from the championship playoffs.

The Royals had a week's layoff before the series and there was a concern that they might grow dull from inactivity. McMahon was determined to prevent this. "To avoid staleness," he said, "we work harder each day in practice." It meant that sometimes he would get in on the scrimmage when one of the players needed a rest. And McMahon and Robertson, playing as if in a championship game, would use tactics that would rile some of the others—and keep them sharp.

Philadelphia had not been easy for the Royals, though they had beaten them 9 out of 12. In those games the Royals had averaged only 3.4 points per game more and three of their wins were by 3 points or less. Now, before a jammed crowd, the two teams traded the lead sixteen times and were tied nine times in the first 7 minutes of the first playoff game. Near the end of the first half, Oscar had taken Neumann close to the basket and his left arm was out in front protecting the ball. Neumann clutched at Robertson's arm and Oscar tried to yank it free. Finally, Robertson threw an elbow and Neumann tumbled back. The two squared off. That's when the benches cleared, with 76er coach Dolph Schayes, face flushed with anger, leading the way.

Embry had taken it upon himself to establish peace. But Gambee—suffering from at least two delusions—thought 1) Embry was attacking and 2) that he might be able to overcome the Cincinnati bull in a show of muscle. But it never came to pass, and the game was soon resumed. The 76ers held a 30-29 lead at the end of the first period. In the second period, with the score tied 44-44, the Royals scored 13 straight points to take a decisive lead. During this period, Costello, guarding Robertson with undue aggressiveness, picked up three quick fouls and left the game never to return. The Royals had a 61-49 halftime advantage.

Lucas, who had sat out much of the rough first quarter with three fouls, made an undeniable impression in the second half, particularly the last quarter, when Philadelphia was rallying. He dominated the boards, scored 15 of his 25 points in the last half and at one point in the fourth quarter made four straight baskets.

The Royals won, 127-102. Robertson had scored 31 points, hitting 8 of 12 from the floor and 15 of 16 free-throw attempts. He also had 16 assists. Lucas, besides his 25 points, had 25 rebounds. One sore spot was Odie Smith. The hustling guard, who had won a starting position by being instrumental in the Royals' twelve-game winning streak, sat out the entire game—except, of course, for the second-period fracas. After the game, when the crowd had gone, Smith came onto the court with a ball and, limply, worked to keep his shooting eye sharp.

The teams had a day of rest before playing at Philadelphia in the second game. And this day, March 23, was a memorable one for Robertson. Newspaper Enterprise Association (NEA), in conjuction with the NBA, annually polls all the players on all the NBA teams to select the Most Valuable Player. (Players cannot vote for members of their own team.) The award is called the Podoloff Cup, named for NBAs' first commissioner.

Oscar Robertson won the award, gathering the widest margin since the poll began in 1956. On the basis of 5 points for first place, 3 for second and 1 for third, Robertson had tallied 362 points. Second was Chamberlain with 215, Russell followed with 167. Robertson had sixty first-place votes to Chamberlain's nineteen and Russell's eleven. Russell had won it the three previous seasons. Chamberlain had won it in 1960, his rookie year. It would be the only time in a nine-year period that someone other than those two tall centers would interrupt as Most Valuable Player. In fact, the only other guard to win at all was Bob Cousy in 1957.

Some of the luster—though not much—was lacking from the award in that earlier in the season the U.S. Basketball Writers' Association had selected their Most Valuable Player. It was Chamberlain, who nosed out Robertson, 235 votes to 225. There was little doubt, though, which was the official designation and which carried the most prestige. The players are really the only people who can determine with authority who the best in the league actually is.

Hal Greer made the difference in the second game. With 6:32 left in the final period he hit a free throw that snapped the game's fifteenth tie and gave Philadelphia a 101-100 lead. Greer hit 9 straight points in this stretch and the 76ers took a 109-100 lead and won. Greer had 15 of his 29 points in the last quarter. In the 122-114 loss, Robertson was the game's high scorer with 30 points, followed by Twyman's 27.

The Royals took a beating in another respect. Both Lucas and Robertson suffered injuries. Robertson's injury was rather minor, though painful. He had a bruised right forearm. Lucas's was more serious. He suffered a sprained lower back in the second period while setting a block for Robertson. He had turned his back on Paul Neumann, who, fighting through the pick, rammed into his back. Though Lucas played the full 48 minutes, he was obviously off form, pulling down but 8 rebounds.

Lucas started the third game of the series, in Cincinnati, but had to leave after the first 4 minutes and 20 seconds.

"I just couldn't jump," said Lucas. In practice the day before, Lucas had worked out and the back gave him only some trouble. "So I thought I'd give it a try in the game," he said. "But every time I moved quickly I felt a sharp stab of pain like a knife in my back. The longer I played the worse it got." It was the second time this season that Lucas had suffered an injury to his back. "The last time I had this injury I was out only one game, but it was three weeks before I was effective again." With Lucas ailing, there was the distinct possibility that the Royals would not have three weeks left this season.

Casualties limped off the floor as often as invective rolled off their tongues, and the fervor was not confined to the court. In the third game, for example, Ike Richman, owner of the 76ers, was expelled from his front-row seat in Cincinnati because he showered verbal abuse upon the referees. On the court, in the same game, Chet Walker did a powwow dance of anger that resulted in a technical foul. McMahon duplicated the dance sometime later—another technical. And in the third period, red-haired Johnny Kerr lost his Irish temper when he took an elbow above the right eyebrow that drew blood. He went after Embry. It was broken up. Kerr left the game and returned in the fourth quarter with three stitches adorning his forehead.

When Lucas left the game the Royals were behind, 16-13. Hawkins replaced him and the Royals spurted to a 13-2 advantage the rest of the quarter and never trailed again. Hawkins was making a big difference. He pulled down 16 rebounds and scored 12 points. "Hawkins has so much spring," said McMahon, "that he could jump over a building."

The first five of Embry, Hawkins, Twyman, Bockhorn and Robertson played the entire second half as the Royals won, 101-89. Embry had 19 rebounds and eleven baskets and, near the end of the game, this graceful dirigible was staggering from fatigue.

Twyman played one of his best games, scoring 21 points and, most remarkably, grabbing 21 rebounds; it was the second-best rebounding game of his career. Bockhorn scored 17 points and held Greer to 18 points—Greer had only six field goals, and only two in first three quarters. Bockhorn's points relieved Robertson of some of the pressure, since he was having a relatively poor night. There are times when, night after night of being double- and triple-teamed, a toll is finally taken. Yet Robertson still scored 28 points and had 12 assists.

Now the Royals led, 2 games to 1. Game four was set for Philadelphia three nights later, Saturday, March 28. On Friday afternoon the Royals held a practice session in Convention Hall. Only eight players drilled. Bud Olsen was out with a sprained ankle. Lucas still suffered from his sprained back. Oscar nursed his bruised forearm. Smith, who had not yet played in the series, was suited up but still not back to full form.

Robertson, after three days off, was expected to be rested

and ready. "You know," McMahon was saying, "Oscar has played good ball the first three games, but he really hasn't busted out yet in the series. You can't fault the guy, though. He's been double- and triple-teamed and pressed every night. They pick him up all over the court. Their strategy is to keep the ball away from Oscar."

Oscar scored 31 points Saturday night. Not enough. Philadelphia won, 129-120, and it was a former University of Cincinnati teammate of Oscar that made the difference. Connie Dierking, the blond 6-9 center, came off the bench to replace Johnny Kerr and scored 16 points in the second half. He had 21 for the game.

Lucas played, though he reinjured his back in the second quarter and his effectiveness was pared. He scored 14 points and had 9 rebounds. But Tom Hawkins, floating through the air, took up the slack. "He is playing," said McMahon, "with dedication." Hawkins had 25 points.

The game did not have an auspicious start for Robertson. He picked up two charging fouls in the first 3 minutes and he and McMahon informed referee Earle Strom that they thought he was in the wrong profession. Oscar was having other problems. At one point in the game he missed 3 of 4 free throws, practically unheard of for him.

For Lucas, the day had one saving grace. He was named Rookie of the Year, an honor that was practically uncontested. During the regular season he had averaged 17.7 points per game, led the league in field-goal percentage with .527 and averaged 17.4 rebounds per game, ranking him third behind Bill Russell and Wilt Chamberlain. He had started for the East in the NBA All-Star game and soon would be named second-team all-NBA.

It had been a fine year for Lucas in many respects but somewhat disappointing in others. He and Robertson would never really hit it off. "At best," said one teammate, after a perspective of several years, "there is a peaceful coexistence."

Lucas had caused more excitement than any other rookie in years, and Robertson must have felt some diminishing of his own premier status. Yet Oscar is a professional and would not let ego eat away at his performance. Robertson knew that, regardless of how good Lucas was, he, Robertson, was still king.

"Lucas is good," said one writer, "but Robertson is the heart of the Royals. They could lose Lucas and still win. If they would lose Robertson, they wouldn't have a chance."

Lucas was unhappy at first that the offense did not go more to him. "The offense isn't set for me," he said, matter-of-factly. "It's set for Oscar. There isn't a single set play for me except at the end of a quarter when we're going for the last shot. And then it's only just that the forward on that side gets the shot and it happens to be me. As a result, my rebounding is more important to me than my scoring."

(Rebounding, like his preoccupation with field-goal percentage, became of great concern to Lucas. Feets Broudy, an eternally smiling, round little man who operates the 24-second clock at Madison Square Garden, tells a story about Lucas. "When I'm working the clock," says Feets, "a lot of players come by and ask me, 'How many points have I got?' Lucas always stops by, too. Only he says, 'How many rebounds have I got?' ")

Lucas had found that when he didn't cut for the ball or try to shake his man, Robertson would not get the ball to him. And there were times when Lucas would go loping downcourt in his easy style, his arms at his sides, his left thumb swallowed in a half-open fist, his right thumb up, the shoulder straps of his uniform rising and falling with each step, his knees perpetually in bandages, and he would get to his spot and stand. In college, he would get to a spot, stand and get the ball. But not in the pros, not with Oscar. "There are times when Lucas stands around counting the house for lack of anything better to do," said one writer.

Oscar has always had an idea that forwards must move to get the ball. Once, Oscar complained about immobility of forwards to McMahon. "I told him," said McMahon, "that he should work with the forwards and I'll take the guards. He showed them how to move, how to use their feet, what kinds of passes to expect from him. In the end, nothing much changed. And I told him, 'The reason they can't do it as well as you, is that you're Oscar, and they're not.'"

There were these times when it appeared Lucas was giving less than his best, that he had other things he was thinking about on the court. Years later a teammate on the 1963-64 Royals said, "I think that that was Jerry's greatest year. He had something to prove then. After that, it became just a job, and a way to build up his name for his outside business ventures." Lucas and his outside business ventures were never very far apart. He had Jerry Lucas basketballs, Jerry Lucas Pass-Time Games, Inc., he owned part of an investment company, some oil wells and would soon go into restaurant ownership. Lucas embodied much of white middle-class America, for all its good and for all its ill. He wanted to be a millionaire by the time he was thirty-five, he had said. And it looked like he was going to make it. This, of course, was not to say that Robertson, the black boy from the slums of Indianapolis, was not also intent upon making a million dollars (the Royals' general manager would be the first to affirm this). But Robertson hungered for a championship. To many, Lucas simply hungered for the dough.

Yet to see the pain with which Lucas played, one had to

suspect that he, too, was a team man who wanted to win. He was now playing with a severely sprained back. And for years he had played with tendonitis in his knees. To strengthen the knees, he built in his basement an exerciser made of weights, pulleys, ropes and two-by-fours. He would sit in a chair and lift his foot dozens of times. Of course, he could not take this exerciser on the road with him, so he improvised. He took a hotel wastebasket, filled it with phone books and assorted handy objects, wrapped a bandage around the basket and lifted it with his foot. "If I can't exercise it every two days," said Lucas, "it hurts."

The ailment developed from Lucas's peculiar jump shot. He bends his right knee in such a way that it crimps the muscles. "For some reason," he said, "the muscles in the upper part of my right leg didn't develop as much as the ones in my left. They don't have the ability to take the strain. It's the only thing I don't like about playing basketball. I've had chronic knee problems for seven or eight years now."

"Luke," said McMahon, "is a hypochondriac." This was several years later and McMahon was recalling that 1964 season. "Look at him on the bench and he's always rubbing his knees. Ask Luke how he is, and you waste half an hour of your day. He tells you he's aching then he goes and pulls down 31 rebounds. You can't be too terribly sore to do that. I kid him about it now."

McMahon, then, was playing Lucas as much as he could, or rather, as much as Lucas could stand it. And McMahon was drawing criticism for it. But McMahon had his answer. "Give a guy a great body like he's got," said McMahon, "and combine it with intelligence and he's not only easy to coach, he's good to be around. Of course, he'll play three good games and the next time sort of stand around. It happens to a lot of players. They tell me maybe he's not hungry enough, why don't you bench him? And I say forget it. Nobody's perfect, but this kid comes close. There was a game against Boston not long ago and he was having a bad one. He was 2 of 17. But there was no way I could take him out. He got 29 rebounds, two more than Russell."

(In the realm of perfection, Lucas's high school trigonometry teacher, Katy Banker, was quoted in *The New York Times:* "If there ever was a God-made man, it's Jerry Lucas. I've never known a boy like him and I don't know when another will come along. He's a once-in-a-lifetime boy.")

Robertson and Lucas were temperamentally different and temperamentally incompatible. They respected each other, and were distant from each other. An entire spectrum of reasons were given for their aloof relationship off the court, everything from race to envy.

"I have to say I don't know Oscar real well," said Lucas. "To know a person real well you would have to spend a heckava lot of time with him." It was hard spending that time with him on the road, for example, because Robertson would be coming out of a restaurant as Lucas entered. Also, Robertson in general is rather distant from all his teammates.

"People made it out to be a racial thing," said Robertson. "That was ridiculous. Look, I don't pal with Odie Smith or Jack Twyman or Arlen Bockhorn, either, and they're white. And I don't pal off the court with Hawkins or Boozer or Thacker, and they're black."

"O and I have had some misunderstandings," said Lucas, "but so have we all with other teammates. But it's like being married. Nothing will run smooth all the time. He and I have come to understand each other. He's an all-right guy."

The series was tied at 2-all now. Each team had won 2 games at home, lost 2 games on the road. They returned to

Cincinnati for the final game. When it wasn't Greer and Neumann and Gambee guarding Robertson, it was Greer and Neumann and Costello, or Bianchi replacing one of them, or Warley switching to him. In the first half of the final game—the game that meant the difference between meeting Boston for the Eastern Division championship—the 76ers knew that they had to stop Robertson to stop the Royals. At the end of the first half the score was tied, 59-59, and Robertson had scored but 6 points. ("All I could see," said Oscar after the game, "were hands.")

In the second half, Bockhorn began to hit from outside (he would finish the game with 23 points). The 76ers had to ease off Robertson—and Robertson went wild. He took nine shots from the field in the second half and made them all. He tried eight free throws and made all of them. Robertson did not miss a shot in the second half, in the most important game of the season up to that point.

The Royals, using an effective fast break, swept to a 74-61 lead. With 5:39 left in the game the 76ers had fought to within 6 points, 112-106. Then Robertson stole the ball from Hal Greer, dribbled across the center line and fed Bockhorn for a layup. Immediately afterward, Robertson blocked a shot by Neumann and was fouled retrieving it. He made the free throws and the Royals had a decisive 9 point lead. The final score was 130-124. Robertson had scored 32 points—13 in the final period—and passed for 18 assists. It was one of his great days. But it was also one of the team's great days. Bockhorn backed up Robertson the way he was expected to. Lucas, still with ailing back and knees, scored 15 points and had 11 rebounds. And again Hawkins was startling; no one plays with his verve. He scored 18 points on 9 of 12 shots from the floor. Twyman had 22 points, Embry was a bulk under the boards. Odie Smith

18

Robertson could not be concerned with his bruised right forearm, regardless of how the pain stabbed him. For this was now the Boston series, something he and the Royals had been pointing to for twelve months, ever since they had nearly upset the Celtics in last year's division finals, losing in the seventh and final game.

And this was the series that Robertson hoped (though he never voiced it publicly) would silence his critics, the ones who said he was not a winner. Bud Olsen had something to say about that. "It's always made me laugh when people say Oscar's not a winner," said Olsen. "I remember them saying it in college. UC's record with Oscar was something like 90 and 9 for three seasons. Can you imagine the star of these kinds of teams being called a loser when his team only loses two or three games a year?"

Of course, the Royals were a better team this season, with the addition of Lucas and the inspirational play—and it really was that—of Tom Hawkins. The team was ailing, however. They had one day off between the last Philadelphia game and the first game in Boston, on Saturday night, March 31. On the Friday before the game the Royals went through a light workout. But before the players went onto the Boston Gardens court, those in lesser fettle lined up for whirlpool treatments. It resembled a breadline during Depression days. Lucas's back needed repair, of course. So did Robertson's arm. Hawkins had a bruised left hand. Olsen still had a sprained ankle. Smith needed heat to help mend his still sore ankle.

On the other side, the Celtics, too, had some physical problems. Frank Ramsey had pulled a thigh muscle in a recent practice session. Heinsohn had just left a sickbed where he had spent three days with the flu. And the Celtics' glowering, sensitive giant, Bill Russell, had ailments of his own. He described them in his autobiography, *Go Up for Glory:*

> 1963-64 was a horrible personal year. I felt the world coming to an end for me. I was on the verge of a nervous breakdown. I could feel everything slipping away from me.
>
> I had to get away, but I was trapped in a world from which there was no escape. No way out. The knees hurt. The pills didn't put me to sleep. The planes always lay one day ahead of us.
>
> It was the long, long season. . . .
>
> How I did it I don't know. But gradually, it ebbed. I woke one morning and the playoffs were beginning and, suddenly, it was all right again and I was whole again. I was Bill Russell again.

Boston had been picked as an 8-5 betting choice in the series, and Auerbach agreed with the odds. First off, he discounted the Royals' regular-season "superiority," in which Cincinnati had beaten Boston 7 times in 12 games. "Don't let that fool you," Auerbach told reporters. "Only one of those games we lost was really important, and we dropped that by a point in overtime.

"We're better prepared for the Royals this year than last. Psychologically, we're better. We've got more respect for them. We were overconfident last season."

Twyman thought that the Celtics' two-week layoff would hurt Boston, though they did practice all but one of those days. "Not playing a game in two weeks has to take some of the edge off them," he said.

Controversies were also being stirred. One involved Havlicek. And he now had to deny remarks attributed to him that Cincinnati, as a town, was odious to him. "I never said that I hate everything about Cincinnati," he said. "That was a bunch of baloney. Sure, I like to do well against the Royals because we lost twice to Cincinnati in the NCAA. Anytime we play I like to beat them."

Russell and Robertson were the center of another discussion. Would Russell be fired up because, being the great and sensitive competitor he was, he was not voted MVP by the players, the honor going to Robertson?

"Let him be fired up, if he is," said Embry. "We've got the MVP on our team."

In the clubhouse, before the first game, Hawkins sat across the room and watched Robertson suit up.

"I'd often watch him dress," said Hawkins. "It was entrancing, almost. I mean, it was never a casual preparation. Everything had to be just so. It was like a religious rite."

Robertson's jersey would be tucked into his shorts with precision. His supporter would be smoothed out. His socks were folded evenly above his sneaker-tops. He would go through maybe five minutes of doing quick exercises before his locker and would handle the ball some, tossing it back and forth in his hand, to get the feel. Oscar, during his dress ritual, is most concerned with his gym shoes. He laces them a special way, taking the laces through the holes from above, rather than the usual pattern of from under.

"I noticed this once," said McMahon, "and I said to Oscar, 'Aha, now I know why you're better than everyone else. You lace your shoes differently!' "

Robertson found that, for him, lacing shoes the everyday way was not acceptable. The shoes were not kept tight enough and his feet were sliding just a bit, which, of course, was too much. So he found a new way to lace his shoes. "I guess it's my own little personal habit," he said.

And now Robertson wanted to make sure everything was absolutely perfect for this game. This season he had played his best ball against the Celtics, the best opponent. He wanted nothing to change.

"Oscar," Lucas had said, "always lifts himself for the big ones. And he always seems to be at his best against the Celtics. Boston is supposed to be the best defensive team in the world, and Oscar gets emotionally pitched to be at his best." For Lucas it was not so easy getting emotionally high. He had to wear a back brace, and this was discouraging.

It was a full house in Boston Garden this Saturday night. For some reason a full house there is always given as 13,909. But there seemed to be more, as people were standing and sitting in the aisles. It was *only* a divisional championship, but the fans knew that it involved the two best teams in basketball. They had come to see if their kings could withstand the ambitions of the pretenders to the throne.

The Celtics, very early, allowed their fans to sigh with relief. They opened a comfortable lead and held a 49-40 halftime advantage and went on to a decisive 103-87 win. It was our worst game of the season," said McMahon.

Some of the Royals who had been hot in the Philadelphia series shot with hands stiff as icicles. Hawkins did not have a basket in eight tries. Bockhorn was 0-for-5 from the field. Lucas, the best field-goal-percentage shooter in the league, had only 4-for-14. And Robertson, who had averaged 31.4 points per game for the season (second to Chamberlain's league-leading 36.9), and who had averaged 33 points a game against the Celtics, was held to 20 points and made just 6 field goals in 20 attempts. In fact, he failed to score a basket in the first 11 minutes of play.

Most of Robertson's scoring came, characteristically, in the second half. But by then the game was moving further and further out of reach for the Royals.

Robertson was harassed every second of the game by the tenacious, relentless K. C. Jones. And when Jones rested, Havlicek took over. Rarely did the Royals throw a pick or a screen, or cut or move. They seemed immobile in the face of the exasperating Celtic defense. Bill Russell scored 18 points, good for him, took down 31 rebounds and either blocked or batted away another ten shots; and when he was doing neither his mere presence made the Royal shooters limp-wristed. The Royals, who again this season had the best team-shooting average in the NBA (.452), could hit on only 31 percent in this big game against Boston.

Their immobility affected the play of their star guard. K. C. and Havlicek in their turns hounded Robertson. The Royals desperately tried to get the ball to him, which turned out to be a chore. And when they succeeded, it seemed they felt their job was over and they stood glue-stiff and observed Robertson try to maneuver into scoring position.

Only Embry had a good night, scoring 21 points and grabbing 16 rebounds against Russell. Still, Russell was so dominating that, when he left the game with 5 minutes remaining, he received a standing ovation from the crowd. At courtside, Pepper Wilson turned to a friend and said, "The man plays the boards like he's a human eraser."

The second game, after a day of rest, was also in Boston. It was a repeat of the first—though, unlike the first, there were times when it appeared the Royals would make a game of it. But it was a mirage. Twyman, who had been sitting and doing much stewing inside, came to life once again. He had not been playing as much as he would have liked, since Hawkins was playing well and McMahon insisted on using Lucas as much as possible. Lucas played 30 minutes in that second game but was inadequate. Because of the pain in his back he could jump only half as high as normally and grabbed but 7 rebounds, made just three free throws and missed all seven attempts from the field.

Twyman, meanwhile, came through with 27 points. He kept the Royals in the game in the first half, scoring 18 points. K. C. Jones again threw a defensive blanket on Robertson. Yet the Royals were able to come from a 29-19 first-quarter deficit and tie the game at 35-all. But then Heinsohn got hot and led a late first-half surge. He scored 18 points in the half, and as the teams left the floor the Celtics led, 50-42. And still the Royals were immobile.

Robertson came into the locker room steaming. This was not unusual when the club was going poorly. He berated the team in general, picking out no one specifically. But in each case they knew who was meant. He said they weren't hustling, that they weren't playing their game. And where were the picks? And they weren't getting back fast enough to stop Boston's fast break.

The Royals pressed in the second half and three times in the last period they pulled to within 9 points. But a Sam Jones jump shot, a Heinsohn hook, a Bill Russell tip, a K. C.

Jones steal always nipped a Royal rally. Heinsohn ended up with the game high of 31 points. Robertson was second with 30. The Celtics won, 101-90, and now the Royals had to win 4 of the remaining 5 games. Not impossible, but not very probable, either.

The locker room of the losers was chillingly silent as the players undressed. McMahon glumly told reporters, "I don't know where our team went."

He was asked which Celtic hurt him the most.

"K. C. Jones, I think he's your star. He was the whole show. He was all over Oscar, he set up the plays, he led the fast break. They beat us," he added, "with aggressive defense and plenty of hustle. We gave up the ball too often, we weren't sharp and we weren't alert. We stood around and held the ball, something you can't do against an aggressive defense. It's ridiculous the way we've been playing. People run around slapping the ball out of our hands and go down the floor and make the basket."

There were now two games in Cincinnati. The fifth, if necessary, would be in Boston, the sixth in Cincinnati, the seventh in Boston. The largest crowd in Cincinnati playoff history and the third-largest in club history, 11,850, squeezed into Cincinnati Gardens for the third game of the series. It had been some nine months since the optimism for a championship year had begun to swell in this town, from the time that Lucas had signed to play, bringing to the club the good big man—no, the great big man—that an NBA title-winner had to have. They began lining up for tickets, these burghers who, uncharacteristically, were letting their hearts instead of their "hard Dutch minds" rule their change purses. And they came, some like pallbearers instead of celebrants, to see for themselves just what kind of devastation was wracking and humiliating their Royals. Hope now hinged on the fact that Boston had won only 1 out of 6 regular-season games they had played at Cincinnati Gardens.

The Royals had a horrendous first half. They shot only 22 percent. Boston hit 49 percent and led at the half, 55-37. In one respect, there was a change in the Royals. After two miserable games, Lucas was playing well, jumping as he had jumped in midseason. "This was after some grumbling among players that Luke should forget his pain for the playoffs since he'll have all summer to rest," wrote one Cincinnati sportswriter.

Lucas scored 14 points (hitting 5 of 17 from the floor), but most impressively he grabbed 24 rebounds, 4 less than Russell. Robertson got 34 points despite K. C. Jones and despite Havlicek. In the second half, Bockhorn hit six straight long jump shots and finished with 18 points.

But the Royals lost their third straight, 102-92.

"And if it hadn't been for Bockhorn," said Auerbach, "we would have won by 25."

Twyman, like almost everyone else on the Royals, was having his problems. "He's giving away more points than he's getting," said McMahon. This could also have been said of Embry, who made but 1 basket in 6 tries, Hawkins, who was 3-for-12, and Smith, who was 0-for-4. Even Oscar's shooting average was off, and he had only 16 assists in the three games, compared with his 11-per-game average during the season.

But game number four would be different.

The Royals had been playing in such a strange way that even K. C. Jones wondered out loud. He had been playing Robertson so close that the only way to effectively get the ball to Oscar would be by lob, since Robertson at 6-5 was 4 inches taller than Jones. "They can just toss it over my head," he said after the third game. "I don't know why they don't do it."

The Royals took Jones's advice, but not right away. They

trailed at the half, 49-46. But in the second half, Embry and Lucas lured Russell outside. This left the lane open for Robertson and he grabbed passes over the head of the smaller Jones and made four straight baskets as the Royals took a 59-57 lead and went on to win.

It was a superb game for the Royals. They broke their shooting slump and they woke up on defense. Robertson was getting some air and he responded with 33 points, 25 of them coming in the second half, which, otherwise, could have been the last half for the entire season. But it was again Oscar at his best when the team needed it, when the season hinged on his performance. Yet, like the season, it was not a one-man show, it never could be, not in the NBA—though Bill Russell, now and then, tried to squelch that theory, and with some success.

It was a grand game for Lucas, too, who out-rebounded Russell, 25-24, and scored 16 points and had 10 assists, several of them to Robertson cutting deep under the basket. And Lucas was healthy in spirit, too. At one point he took a wild swing at Heinsohn, who had let an elbow run amuck. Twyman was also tough, with 31 points.

"They're not a punk club that you can beat four times in a row," said Auerbach. "They have a lot of pride."

"Our key guy was Luke," said McMahon. "I thought he wanted it real bad."

The teams returned to Boston for the fifth game. The Celtics could afford to breathe easier, since they had to win but 1 of the next 3 games. The Royals had to fight for air. Yet they were relatively loose. In the locker room, Robertson joked with Embry and said hello to "Enoch Light," who was, in this case, Bud Olsen. Olsen's given first name is Enoch (and Enoch Light is an orchestra leader).

Staverman and Robertson rehashed an old familiar needle. Staverman and Yvonne Robertson are both from Covington,

Kentucky. Robertson tells Staverman that his wife was a hillbilly until he civilized her. The intimation is that Staverman is still unreconstructed mountainfolk. Then Staverman would counter with an example of Robertson's penchant for penny-pinching. Yvonne's father owned a dry-cleaning store in Covington. Staverman would needle Oscar that he got married just so he could get his cleaning free.

"Oscar was relaxed before big games," recalls Embry. "And the rest of us picked it up. We said to ourselves, well, if the greatest is relaxed, then we should be, too. In ways like this, he made us all better ballplayers."

It was not long before omens became ominous for Cincinnati. The Royals were leading, 8-7, and Lucas had scored half their points. But then, while driving for the basket, Lucas fell over K. C. Jones and landed hard on the back of his head and left elbow. He lay there writhing under the basket as the trainer came rushing out and the players moved quietly nearby. Lucas was shaken, but rose and said he would continue. And he did, but not as earlier— making only 1 out of 7 shots.

He was finally taken out at the end of the third period.

"That fall took the spunk out of me," he would say later. "I think I chipped my elbow."

In that first period, Robertson made one of the most sensational, most outrageously surprising shots of his career. There was a switch and Russell suddenly was guarding Robertson about 8 feet to the left of the basket. Robertson took that hard thumping dribble of his, stopped, dropped into a crouch as though he were going to spring for his jump shot but instead remained for a short but seemingly eternal second in that crouch. Russell was not sure what was developing. Then Robertson shot, from right there in that crouch, and the ball went in.

Going back downcourt, Russell was cackling under his

beard. For he thought it was funny as well as marvelous and loped alongside Robertson and said, "You gotta be kidding me."

Russell continued having a good time. It was becoming funereal for Robertson, however. The Celtics led at the end of the first quarter, 33-19. Heinsohn sparked the surge with 12 points, including two long sweeping hook shots that had the crowd raising the roof beams.

Nothing much changed during the rest of the game. As had been the case throughout the series, Robertson was surrounded by K. C. Jones or Havlicek virtually every second he was on offense. And there was Russell the colossus. He scored 20 points, had 7 assists and smothered the boards for 35 rebounds. He was the difference. A Dayton, Ohio, sportswriter said, "Oscar has more grace and speed and shooting ability than Russell. Certainly Oscar is more thrilling to watch and perhaps it can be argued of greater talent, but Oscar never saw the day when he can dominate a game as Russell."

And maybe it is so. Surely if the records are any barometer, it is unquestioned. The Celtics won, 109-95, and won their eighth straight divisional championship. Soon they would play San Francisco, which had defeated St. Louis, 4 games to 3 for the NBA championship. It would be almost no contest. Russell would have it all over Chamberlain, too. Boston would win its seventh title in eight years, and Russell, before retiring in 1969, would go on to lead Boston to eleven NBA championships in the thirteen years he played for them. A record unparalleled in professional team sports of any kind.

Robertson, in his final game of the season, scored 24 points, but made just 8 of 22 from field. He had 9 rebounds and 8 assists. He was very disappointed. And he sat sullenly with head down and hands clasped between his legs as

McMahon talked to the club after the game, keeping the press out for fifteen minutes.

McMahon told the team that, despite this playoff, they had had a great year. He complimented the players on hustling all season long. He said that he had no prima donnas and that the club had good harmony. But that the Royals had gotten off to a bad start with Boston, and it was injuries suffered against Philadelphia that hurt them as much as anything. But Boston had played sensationally, he said, applying pressure and forcing us into errors. They hustled and could've beaten anybody.

Then he paused. He was as disappointed as they were, yes, and, well, how do you sum up a season in which you have done better than you've ever done before, and, finally, were beaten by a clearly superior team. What do you say to sum up the long months of living together, playing together, waiting for planes in the dead of night together, missing your wives and families together, feeling your muscles ache as one, and your eyes straining to shut as one, and sharing too the hope that now, this season, after games and games and games, interminable it seemed, fatiguing to the extreme, that at the end together you will be champions. Now you had lost. The dream was shattered. What do you say to sum it up?

"I have nothing but pride in this team," McMahon told them, just before giving the okay to let the reporters in.

So now it was over for Robertson, too. He could draw some consolation in the season, but again much of it would be personal. He was again, of course, named to the first-team all-NBA squad, along with Pettit, Chamberlain, Baylor and West. He was named professional athlete for the month of March in the Hickok Belt award. K. C. Jones would praise Robertson and then, amid a group of sportswriters, say he was sorry for the way he had guarded Robertson. "I don't like to play a man like that—all over the court when he doesn't have the ball. It's like cheating. It isn't fair to him." But fairness is not necessarily compatible with professionalism in sports. The objective is to win, to win within the rules if you have to, but win any way you can.

Robertson had said a similar thing. "That sportsmanship stuff is fine," he said. "But winning is all that matters. Because they haven't stopped keeping the score yet. You get no points for sportsmanship."

Robertson's career from college days on has been filled with personal glories of every kind, yet a professional championship continued to elude him, and, it seemed, always would, until he was traded to Milwaukee in 1970 and would team with 7-footer Lew Alcindor.

Pro Basketball has been dominated by the big man, from the beginning of the NBA, when George Mikan was the scourge and Minneapolis won title after title. Later, Pettit's St. Louis Hawks were the primary threat, followed by Russell's Celtic reign—to be broken only twice in thirteen years: once by Pettit and the Hawks when Russell was injured, and once by Chamberlain, who played to his potential.

Lucas has turned out to be a fine pro—some say he is the best rebounding foward in professional basketball history. But somehow he is not the man to turn the tide of a championship game. (Lucas was traded to San Francisco in 1969.) Nor is it enough to be like Robertson, the best playmaker, best offensive threat from guard, best rebounding guard, best all-around everything—it is not enough in the NBA if you stand only 6 feet 5 inches.

Robertson says that "it's not the end of the world" not to be on a championship team. But Yvonne, his wife, knows that it gnaws at him. She knows he was terribly frustrated that he was on second-best teams.

"He doesn't voice these things," she said, "even to me. But I have the impression that he's competing against himself now even more than against another player or team. Just to see how much better he can be, how he can do something a little differently and still do it well. Just to keep accomplishing and improving."

Robertson continues to pursue personal excellence, just as he did when he was a boy in the Indianapolis ghetto and his older brothers kicked him out of the Dust Bowl and told him to play someplace else, and he practiced by himself, telling himself that someday he would be better than all of them. But it is not enough. It is the championship that he craved.

There was the night, after the third Celtic playoff game, that comes to mind. The game was over, the Royals had lost their third straight. One more and they would be finished. Oscar Robertson came out of the clubhouse, alone. The corridor leading to the back door of Cincinnati Gardens was dark and deserted on this night. Robertson pulled up the collar of his raincoat. He tugged his hat down firmly on his head and strode out into the rain, determined that in the next game he would lead his team to victory, determined that he would be part of a championship. This elegance and tenacity, sometimes muddling his thoughts but always driving him on—these are the qualities that have made Oscar Robertson the best at what he does, and these qualities have prodded him to do better, on and off the court, next quarter, next day. And as in the poem by Dylan Thomas, Oscar Robertson does not go gentle into that good night. He rages, rages, against the dying of the light.

THE GOLDEN YEAR SERIES

❦   ❦   ❦

The Golden Year Series consists of books devoted to the most spectacular year in the careers of America's outstanding athletic figures. In addition to Oscar Roberston, other sports greats featured in this series are: Joe DiMaggio, Jim Brown, Frank Gifford, Jack Dempsey, Ted Williams, and Arnold Palmer.